Tied With Red Cord

Unraveling My Grandmother's Story

Margaret Lenton Hale

This story is for my mother, Marion, and for Margaret, who were unable to tell it,

For my sister, Wendy, and for me, who uncovered it,

And for our children and grandchildren who now will know it.

A decade of research went into compiling this story. The timeline can be documented, and the letters speak for themselves. Scenes are based on fact, but have been enhanced by my imagination.

The letters Becky handed me were tied together with a red cord. I later asked her if that was the way she found them in her grandmother's attic. "Yes," she said "...tied with red cord."

...

I have a memory of standing near the kitchen sink one evening as Mother and I were doing dishes and asking her about her family. Armed with a pen and notebook, I was gathering information for a class assignment geared to determine my heritage. She informed me that I came from English and Norwegian stock, and that there might have been one great grandmother who was Irish.

Little more was said about her family.

...

Chapter 1

Summer 1997

I felt a sense of adventure as Wendy and I headed south from Hudson, Wisconsin, to Southeastern Minnesota. Wendy was visiting from her home in Seattle without her husband, and just the two of us were off to visit family and friends and to spend time together, something we sisters had never done before.

We had decided to spend one night in Lanesboro, the small town where our mother had spent her early childhood years, a place neither of us had visited for some time. In recent years Lanesboro had gained attention because of its restaurants, shops, and bed & breakfast establishments.

We had booked a night at Mrs. B's, a B&B started by our former neighbor (Mr. B), and were heading there on Highway 52 when we saw a sign at the town of Fountain directing us left to Lanesboro.

"Lanesboro is that way," said Wendy, pointing left.

It wasn't the route I had planned to take, but I turned, and just around the corner we encountered the Fillmore County Museum.

"Shall we stop?" I asked.

"Let's," said Wendy.

Getting out of the car, she told me to grab my genealogy books. I had dabbled in family history for many years and had brought the books along in case we went to any cemeteries or places that might give me more information.

We entered the museum expecting to look at the artifacts, but the woman at the desk cast her eyes on the papers I was carrying.

"I have some genealogy papers with me," I explained.

"Follow me to the research room,' she commanded, leading the way.

Feeling awkward about the situation, Wendy and I followed her down the hall.

"They are interested in genealogy," she instructed the woman in the room.
Immediately we were cast into an unexpected situation.

The woman in charge was very friendly and eager to show us how to use the filing system.

"We have obituaries, birth records, newspapers, and microfiche," the woman explained. "What would you like to see?"

We stood dumbfounded, not knowing what to say.

"Well, let me show you how the system works," she said. "Do you know anyone who was born in this county?"

"Our mother," we replied.

We gave her our mother's birth date, and she retrieved some microfiche and fed the tape into the machine. Scrolling down a birth record, she came to the Dent name.

We strained to make out the hand-written ledger that appeared on the screen and to scan the columns searching for our mother's name. There it was - Marion Cordelia Dent. We traced across

the line to see her mother's name, but instead of
Carrie Dent, it read Margaret G. Dent.

We looked at each other and then in unison,
told the woman that this was wrong. Margaret was
mother's oldest sister. Their parents were Milton
and Carrie Dent.

Then we looked at each other and my sister
said, "Do you suppose?"

We ran our fingers across the screen again,
stopping under the column that recorded the
father's name. It took some effort to decipher the
handwriting and reveal the clearly Scandinavian
name that we had never seen or heard.

Again, we both turned to the woman and told
her that something was wrong, that this
information wasn't right.

"Sometimes there are mistakes in these
records," the woman said. "Let's check it against
a census report." And she went to retrieve the
information. She returned with the 1910 census on
microfiche and again threaded the film into the
machine.

We found the Dent family: Milton, head of the
household; Carrie, his wife; their children –

Margaret, Clarence, Agatha, Elvina, and Charlotte. Listed last was Marion - *granddaughter.*

"Do you think?" asked Wendy, looking at me.

"This can't be," I said. Margaret had always been "Aunt Margaret," and she had spent her final years living with our family.

I felt a rock drop into my stomach, and my sister sank back on her chair. Wait a minute - had we just learned that the people our mother called "mother" and "father" were in fact her grandparents? Did the birth record correctly record that Margaret, the woman we always thought was mother's oldest sister, was in fact her mother and our grandmother?

...

Margaret – "Aunt Margaret" – was our grandmother? How could that be? She had spent her final years in our house, mostly bedridden with diabetes and congenital heart disease … and we didn't know that she was our grandmother?

My memory of her is foggy as she died shortly before my sixth birthday, but I do remember her. I also know that my name "Margaret" was to honor her. But she was my grandmother? Mother had always told us that her parents were Milton and Carrie Dent, and both of them had died before either Wendy or I was born.

Our father's mother – our Grandma Aletta – lived on a farm a mere five miles from us. She was very much a part of our family, and Wendy and I loved her as a grandmother.

But Margaret had been just "Aunt" Margaret - an aunt like the many other aunts we had.

...

The woman at the museum who was helping us appeared to be as shaken as we were, but at our request, she went to a file and looked up the name of the man who had been listed as our mother's father.

She returned with an obituary of the man, a sad tale of a 30-year-old who died of the Spanish flu epidemic while serving in World War I. He had been the first war casualty from his hometown of Lanesboro and a lengthy obituary paid him homage. He left behind a young wife and a two-month-old son.

"There's a notation here that says his photograph is on his gravestone," said the woman. "He's buried in the local cemetery."

...

We read the obituary with great interest:
PRIVATE QUARSTAD LAID TO REST
Private Oscar Alvin Quarstad came home Sunday, and in the Lanesboro cemetery there was a new made grave to receive the first lad from this community to make the supreme sacrifice for his country and the great cause of world liberty.
The funeral took place early Monday morning. Complying with regulations of the state board of health the ceremonies had to be simple and brief. Under dull leaden skies a large number gathered outside the undertaking establishment. The Lanesboro Band rendered a funeral dirge, as the flower bedecked coffin was carried out and placed in the hearse. Rev. P.J. Nestande, standing on the steps, delivered a short eulogy of the dead soldier lad, and then the last sad journey to the grave: the Stars and Stripes - carried by a Civil War veteran, Mr. P. Nelson Viklund - flying over the hearse; the

*band playing "Nearer My God to Thee,"
preceding it, and the family of the deceased
following it in a carriage. At the grave "taps"
were sounded by Mr. S.L. Fosse.*

*As a mark of respect to Lanesboro's first
soldier dead every business place in town was
closed during the funeral.*

*That the deceased was beloved by his comrades
was evident from the fact that his company had by
telegraph ordered a splendid floral piece - a pillow
of immense white chrysanthemums and beautiful
pink roses with the inscription, "From Co. A, 25th
B'n."*

*And so, Private Quarstad was buried. In the
years to come his resting place in Lanesboro's
beautiful God's acre will be visited again and
again by loved ones, who will cherish his memory
and strew upon the sleeping dust fragrant flowers
mingled with tears of affection.*

*Oscar Alvin Quarstad was born in Lanesboro
August 28, 1887. He enlisted as a volunteer in his
country's service immediately after the declaration
of war in April last year. First he was stationed at
Camp Cody, New Mexico; then in September last
year transferred to Presidio, California, and later*

to Camp Taliaferro, at San Diego, where he was assigned to coast guard duty. Here he was taken ill and died October 6th, a victim of the influenza epidemic. He died while in camp, but - as Rev. Nestande said in the funeral sermon – 'the soldier who makes the sacrifice for his county while in training is entitled to equally as much credit for fortitude, patriotism and courage as is the one who meets his fate on the field of battle.'

On June 9th, 1917, at Austin, the young soldier, while back on furlough, was married to Miss Cora Olson of Houston (Minn.). To them were born a couple of months ago a baby boy, who never will see his father. Besides his young wife and baby he also leaves his parents, Mr. and Mrs. Odin Quarstad, three brothers, and four sisters. One brother, Private Arnold Quarstad, is now at Camp Hancock in Georgia.

The hearts of the community go out in deepest sympathy to the wife, parents, sisters and brothers of the deceased. In their great loss they too have made their great contribution to their country, the sacrifice which surpasses all others.

...

We left the museum shaken and mystified, stopped to have some lunch, and mulled over what we had just learned. Then we headed up the hill to the picturesque cemetery that overlooks the little bluff-country town. My sister and I split up and began walking between the rows of gravestones. About three-quarters of the way through the cemetery, she shouted that she had located Margaret's grave. I turned to head back to her when a headstone with a small American flag next to it caught my eye. There was the other name we were searching for. I saw that there was an oval-shaped photograph attached, but didn't stop to look at it, sensing that we needed to share that moment.

We studied Margaret's headstone and those of her mother and sister nearby and then moved two rows over to confront the picture of Oscar Quarstad, the man who was our grandfather.

The man in the photograph had a handsome, angular face, but it was the eyes that caught our attention. They were deep set and surrounded by darkened circles…

Just like our mother's eyes.

Oscar Alvin Quarstad   Marion Cordelia Dent

My back was to her and I thought she was sleeping, but then she blurted out "Do you think our mother knew this story?"

My answer was that if she had known, she would have told us.

It was strange sharing a bedroom with my sister. We hadn't done that since we were young. But here we were, middle aged, at Mrs. B's Bed & Breakfast in Lanesboro, Minnesota. The room was decorated in the flavor of the turn-of-the century building that housed it: salmon colored, flowered-wallpaper, Victorian table and chairs, and twin beds with tall, ornately carved headboards and bed frames.

Mr. B., (Jack Bratrud), had grown up across the street from Wendy and me in Stewartville, Minnesota, and the inn he and his wife had created had gained renown for its accommodations and fine dining. That afternoon, while enjoying ice cream cones on Lanesboro's main street, we had run into Mrs. B., Nancy, also a long-time acquaintance. The Bratruds no longer owned the inn, but Nancy was curious as to which room we were occupying. Hearing it was the room with the twin beds, she informed us that Jack had done the carving on the headboards and bed frames.

But that night, even the beautiful beds couldn't lull us into sleep. Events of the day and questions upon questions raced through our heads.

The unanticipated stop at the county museum had unraveled our Mother's family history. Our world had been rocked.

We twisted and turned in the beds with the lovely carvings, fluffing our pillows, rearranging the covers.

"Why do you think no one ever told us this story," asked Wendy.

"I don't know. Do you think Dad knew?"

"Wouldn't he have told us after Mother died?"

"What about our aunts and uncles - why didn't any of them ever say something?"

Questions and speculation about what might have taken place reverberated around the quaint room into the early hours of morning before sleep finally overtook us.

I awoke to sunshine flooding the room, the

light turning the salmon colors even more vibrant, jolting me to the realization of the story uncovered yesterday.

Chapter 2

On our way back to Hudson from Lanesboro we stopped in Rochester and called our "cousin" Geraldine (daughter of Elvina, one of Margaret's sisters) and asked if we could stop to see her. We shared what we had discovered, and she told us that she knew the story, that she was told sometime in her teens that her mother was not our mother's sister. She seemed surprised that we had never known the truth.

In her working days, Geraldine had been a secretary at city hall in Rochester. We often ran into her on the streets of Rochester as city hall was in the heart of the shopping district. Geraldine was a fashion plate – she was trim, and her blond hair was always well coiffed. I can still see her in a stunning red outfit – a slim skirt with a cape jacket. My mother always referred to her as her "niece," when in fact they were cousins.

All these years we had called Margaret's sisters, Elvina, Agatha, and Charlotte, our "aunts'

when, in fact, they were our mother's aunts and
our great aunts. All of them, along with their
brother, our "Uncle" Clarence, and all their
spouses were dead, and so were their stories.

...

A few days after our visit with Geraldine, she
wrote to Wendy saying she had talked with her
sister, Mildred, and they were both surprised that
we didn't know that Margaret was Mother's
mother. She wondered if Mother, herself, knew –
if her other so-called "sisters" knew. What about
our dad?

*"I know the family dearly loved her as their own
sister,"* wrote Geraldine. *"We did, too. We
always called her our Aunt Marion. I remember
Mom always telling about Marion when she was
real little – they were out walking – going up a hill
– Marion said 'carry dis little bird, I's too tired to
walk.'"*

Thoughts of Margaret flooded my mind in the
ensuing months. I strained to remember what I
could about her. The most vivid memory was that

of her bedroom (which later became mine). On the wall was a small black wooden cross with a white plastic Jesus.

Beside her bed was a three-tiered narrow table. On its top shelf were a green glass water carafe with a tumbler that fit over its neck, a rosary, a small black case that held a hypodermic syringe, the book that Margaret was currently reading, her Bible, her wire glasses, and a small knife with an ivory handle that she told me "had belonged to a man who died in a war."

...

Mostly I remember "Aunt" Margaret in bed in the small bedroom at the top of the stairs, but there are a few blurred memories of her in the kitchen of our house.

I had an idyllic childhood - making tents with Wendy, either by slipping a blanket over the clothesline, or by putting up two card tables and arranging blankets over them; playing with toys in a corner of the basement where a rug had been laid to cover the cold concrete floor; riding a tricycle up and down the sidewalk, sometimes with my first friend, Susan, whose mother would help her cross the street at the end of the block, and many trips to Grandma's farm a mere five miles away.

It was common practice in the '40s and '50s for high school girls who lived in the country to room with families in town, exchanging childcare and house cleaning for room and board. Doris lived with our family in a time I do not remember, but I do remember Leona spending her high school years with us. We lived only a block from the high school, so it was a perfect situation for Leona who wanted to take part in extracurricular activities. I remember tagging along with her and her neighborhood friends, Audrey and Belva, on trips to Berg Drug where they drank Cokes at the long soda fountain counter.

Me with Leona

When I was a child, our house had a front porch that was enclosed with screening, but later my parents had the screening removed. In addition to the front door, the house had two other doors: the back door that we used most often as it was near the garage, and a side door, used almost exclusively by my dad. He came through that door at lunch time and after a day of work as manager of the local grain elevator, usually paused outside to roll down his pant cuffs and shake out the bits of grain, corn or soybeans that had collected there.

When I was very young, the milkman also used that door. He would step into the small landing and set the glass bottles of milk along a ledge of the three steps that led up to the kitchen.

Our yard was not large, but it was just the right size for making snowmen, snow angels and snow forts in the winter, for running through the sprinkler on hot summer days, and for making leaf houses in the fall. The house had a simple plan: a living room, dining room with a very small adjoining room, and kitchen downstairs and three bedrooms and a bathroom upstairs. An open stairway on one end of the living room led to the upstairs; a dark brick fireplace surrounded by white bookcases anchored the opposite end of the room. Above the bookcases on either side of the fireplace were small stained-glass windows that created wonderful color patterns at sunset.

Built in the 1920s, the house was heated with hot water, so there were radiators in each of the rooms. They were great places to set wet mittens or to warm up socks before putting them on. In the living room, under the triple window, was a long, low radiator where you could sit to really get warmed up. If you sat on it while you were wearing a dress, you could count on having red streaks up the back of your legs when you walked away.

The dining room was dominated by three windows in a bay area that gave way to a view down the hill to the park.

...

It was while Leona was with us that "Aunt" Margaret came to live with us. A former nurse, she was single, and in ill health. Sometimes she would call me to her small room, and we would listen to "Big John and Little Sparky" on the radio.

I would sit on the floor next to the warm radiator upon which she placed halves of orange peels that permeated the room with a fresh citrus scent.

Margaret was a Catholic while we were Lutherans from a long line of Lutherans. She received many visits from Fr. Mountain, the local Catholic priest, and from Dr. Risser, the only doctor in Stewartville. I liked Fr. Mountain - he was always friendly to me. Dr. Risser was friendly, too, but it seemed that any time he was called to see me I received a shot of some kind. When I was four, he removed my tonsils at the hospital in Austin, and memories of that caused me to like him even less, to the point that if I saw him coming up the front steps, I would hide.

Wendy remembers Margaret as being "enormous," full of fluid. She said Dr. Risser made visits to drain her body of that fluid.

Ours was a busy house with two children, a high school student, a woman in her late 50's with major medical problems, and my parents in their mid to late 30s.

...

Shortly after learning my true relationship to Margaret, I sent a Christmas card to Leona telling what I had discovered. A few days later she called, expressing disbelief at the story.

"Margaret was so patient in the face of her illness," she said. "She was gentle, happy, and didn't complain. I remember that she was on a strict diet of 800 calories a day. Lunch would be bullion soup.

"During the years that she was still working as a nurse at Wadena, Minnesota, at a tuberculosis center," she recalled, "your mother wrote regularly to her. I remember taking letters to the post office.

"Your mother never went to visit her at Wadena and Margaret never came to visit in Stewartville. She came when she got ill. It was a heart condition and she had lots of fluid buildup."

Leona was truly mystified that their relationship had never come to light.

•••

My parents moved to Stewartville, Minnesota, two months before I was born. It must have been an exciting time for them: a second baby on the

way, the first house they would own, and a new
management position for my dad. By then they
had been married for eight years, and those first
eight years had been spent in Kasson, another
small southeastern Minnesota town about thirty
miles from Stewartville. My dad had managed the
local grain elevator there, and my mother had
given up a teaching career to become a housewife,
and then a mother, caring for my six-year-older
sister, Wendy. Now my dad was to be the
manager of a larger grain elevator in his
hometown.

...

Stewartville was home, not only to my dad, but
also to his father, Robert Lenton, and to his
father's parents. My great-grandparents Charles
and Caroline Lenton, came from England. How
they happened to end up in Stewartville remains a
mystery, but a crumbling, slightly tipped
tombstone in Woodlawn Cemetery stands
testimony to their life there.

...

Leona was off to college when I started kindergarten. Because the school building, only a block from our house, was overcrowded, I went to kindergarten in the Stewartville Community Building. Four blocks from our house it required a walk through the business district and across Main Street, so my mother left Margaret and made the two daily trips with me. I was glad she was with me as I had an intense fear of dogs at that age.

I wore dresses to school each day and particularly remember a green plaid dress with a white Peter Pan collar and black, patented leather belt, pretty much like the dress of every other girl in the class. In winter I wore slacks under my dress and tucked the legs into my overshoes (or galoshes) that had metal buckles on them.

I remember mornings when I fussed about the way my socks felt. The little line across the top of the toes had to be just right so that when I put on my shoes there was no bunching. I would throw tantrums about my socks while Margaret lay ill in the next room.

Sometimes Margaret was able to be downstairs and she would sit at the kitchen table with us where she would admonish me to eat the bread crust because it "would make my hair curly."

...

My grade school years passed happily, most of them in the same 1900 square brick building my dad had attended and where my mother had taught, just a block from our house. I walked to the school, came home for lunch and walked back again. I was usually accompanied by my friend, Susan, who lived across the street at the end of the block, Sam, whose house we passed on the way, and Tim and Dan who walked up a block from near the park to meet us. However, due to overcrowding, my fourth grade class met in the rod and gun club building a few miles from town. I still walked to the brick schoolhouse, but then boarded a bus to the country site. I loved school, my teachers, my friends and the activities. My mother, who had been a teacher, was a "housewife" during those years and was home when I came for lunch and when I returned at the end of the school day. My dad was the mayor of Stewartville for many years and was very involved in civic and church affairs. He wore tan pants and a tan shirt to work at the elevator, but if he had a meeting at night, he showered and put on a white shirt, a tie, and a sport coat. And he always wore a hat.

Mother, too, was involved in church and PTA and belonged to several bridge clubs. I loved it when bridge club was meeting at our house: It always meant there would be a special dessert in the refrigerator. In those days, playing cards required dressing up. Mother and her friends wore dresses, high heels and lots of colorful costume jewelry. Dad, Wendy and I would be banned to the upstairs of the house where we could hear the soft conversation, the slapping of cards and occasional squeals of astonishment when a good play was made.

Before I entered school, I went along with Mother to Ladies Aid and Mission Circle at Zion Lutheran Church where cake, coffee, and Kool Aid usually were served after a meeting. My Grandma Aletta (Dad's mother) would be there, too. On Sundays she and her second husband, Fred, would be seated on the left-hand side of the sanctuary. Zion Lutheran Church, only a block from our house, was a major part of my family's life, and we participated in most activities there.

•••

Margaret is my given name, yet I've never gone by it.

As a child, it embarrassed me. It was an "old lady's" name, and I grew up in an era when "cute' names were the fad. My classmates had names like Sally and Patty and Kathy. "Peggy" suited me much better.

But as I've grown older, the name has slowly become a part of my identity. Because it's my legal name, it's the one I use in my signature, so now store clerks, telemarketers, and the receptionists at doctors' offices and dentists' offices call me "Margaret." I used to look around for the "Margaret" they were calling, but now I know I am that Margaret.

•••

I've always known that I was named for the person my mother called "her oldest" sister,"

Margaret Grace Dent. She however, was
christened "M-a-r-g-e-r-e-t-t". I suspect she was
named for her father's mother, Margaret Fowler
Dent, but that the spelling maybe was a concession
to her mother's Scandinavian roots. At some point
in her life, she reverted to spelling her name in the
traditional manner. Was it too inconvenient to
have an unusual spelling or did she change it to
distance herself from the family?

...

Margaret's paternal grandmother, Margaret
Fowler Dent, was born in Maryland in 1829 and
attended a girls' school in Baltimore. She married
Dr. Walter Brewer Dent (son of Levi and Pamelia
Dent), a physician, and they came to Wisconsin in
1854. They returned to Maryland for a short time,
but then resettled in Portage, Wisconsin in 1862.

At the age of forty, Margaret Fowler Dent was
widowed and left with seven children under the
age of fourteen – May, Minnie, Hewitt, Milton
(Margaret's father, my great grandfather),
Warring, Cecil and Brewer. I am curious how she

managed financially during her long life of eighty-seven years.

On a trip to Portage to do some family research, I discovered a city directory from the early part of the century. Margaret Fowler Dent's name and address were listed so I walked to that address which was on a street one block behind the town's business district. A Masonic Hall stood on the plot where her house would have been. Flanked by large, gracious old homes, it was not hard to imagine that Dr. Dent and his family could have lived in a similar house, and that he might have had his medical office on the main floor.

...

Margaret's father, Milton Jerome, the fourth child of Walter Brewer and Margaret Fowler Dent, was born in Portage, Wisconsin. He left that area and settled in Milwaukee, according to an 1880 census, which listed the 19-year-old as a fireman in a railroad shop. Soon after that he came to Southeastern Minnesota. For years I had heard rumors that he had been married before he married Margaret's mother, Carrie A. Ellingson, and through census records, I was able to confirm that he did, indeed, have a first wife, Eunice Quinn (born in Ohio, but a Minnesota resident at the time of their marriage) and that a daughter, Frannie, was born in 1886.

Four years later, he married Carrie.

Carrie was the daughter of Norwegian immigrants, Gilbert and Kari Bergsrud Ellingson, who came to the United States in 1857. After eleven years in Wisconsin, Gilbert and Kari settled in Pilot Mound, Minnesota, near Lanesboro. Carrie was the second of their six children. In her young adulthood she worked on a farm near Chatfield, the town where Milton and his first family lived. Census records show that she lived in the home of Mr. and Mrs. Arthur Ecker and their 13-year-old son. Also living in the home were two boarders (one a day laborer, the other a brakeman), and three servants - Carrie undoubtedly numbered among them. Carrie was nearly 29 (a late age for the time) when she married Milton, 28. The daughter of Norwegian Lutherans, she married a divorced Catholic. Their daughter, Margaret, arrived eight months after they

were married. I can only speculate that Carrie
might have married to conceal a pregnancy.

...

Wendy was already in the upper elementary
grades when I was in kindergarten, and doing very
"grownup" things in my eyes. She and her friends
were playing in the park and making Indian camps
in the reeds along Lake Florence. One year at
Christmas time, she played Mrs. Santa Clause in
the elementary school program, complete with a
red cotton skirt trimmed with cotton batting. I sat
with Mother in the balcony of the gym dreaming
of the day when I might be able to play such a part.

During this time, Aunt Margaret grew more ill
and Dr. Risser had her admitted to St. Olaf
Hospital in Austin. I have a memory of Wendy
and me going there with our parents and the two of
us sitting in a waiting room while they went to see
her. We were later told that Margaret wanted to
see us, and we were allowed (as children usually
weren't) into a dim room where she lay in a
hospital bed that seed extremely tall to me. She
died February 26, 1952, at the age of sixty.

Her obituary:

Miss Margaret Dent
Funeral Service Held

STEWARTVILLE – Funeral services were held here today for Miss Margaret Grace Dent, who died Tuesday at an Austin hospital after a long illness. She was 60 years old. Burial was in the Lanesboro cemetery.

Miss Dent was born May 10, 1891 at Preston. She attended Lanesboro public school and took nurse's training at Mount Pleasant, Iowa.

Surviving is one brother, Clarence J. Dent of La Crosse, Wis.; four sisters, Mrs. Elaine (Elvina) *Austin of Chatfield, Miss Agatha Dent of Rochester, Mrs. Matthew Darr of Austin, and Mrs. Wendell Lenton of Stewartville.*

Me with Wendy

Chapter 3

I was almost six, but have no memory of a funeral. I only know that her room at our house was cleared out and that my tiny youth bed was moved into it. Margaret's water carafe was stored in one of the glass-door cupboards in the dining room, and her many books, her glasses, and the little knife in the ivory holder, pieces of Margaret that my mother could not discard, were placed in the bookshelves that flanked our fireplace. A large green metal trunk tucked in the walk-in closet of our bathroom held her nursing hat, some pictures, a long chain (which Mother had said Margaret wore around her waist to hold keys for the rooms at the state institutions where she had worked), and the black wooden crucifix with the plastic Jesus. I used to love to look at the contents of that trunk - old time photos of Margaret as a nursing student and one where she is posing very seriously, horn-rimmed glasses on her nose and a starched nursing cap on her head. There were also a few other pictures of the Dent family, including several of my mother as a baby. Some of my mother's baby pictures were on post cards, addressed to Margaret. An early picture card addressed to Margaret in care of Lutheran Hospital in La Crosse bears this inscription *"Dear Sister Margaret, Here I am at last, slow but sure. We are all well and so is Marion. Well, guess I'll have to close. From Marion."*

Another one notes *"Here is Marion in the dress you sent her,"* and yet another describes Marion – *"hair almost black, eyes black, strip of light blue on collar, dress faint lavender."*

The black wooden crucifix with the plastic
Jesus intrigued me. We Lutherans didn't have
such religious artifacts. I liked to hold it and look
at it.

···

The small bedroom at the top of the stairs
where Margaret had lain was mine for the next
seven years. It was a comforting room located
between my parents' bedroom and Wendy's
bedroom. I loved the double windows that looked
out on to the side lawn and gave a view a block
down to the lake. The room also had a large walk-
in closet with a ceiling that slanted with the
roofline.

···

Our house had no locks.
There was no need for dead bolts or security
systems during my childhood years. In the midst
of the Midwest winter, the front door with the oval
glass in it was our insulation against the cold and
whatever else lurked in the darkness. On humid,
still summer nights, we merely put the hook of the
porch screen door through the eye and left the

heavy inner door open in hopes that some breeze would find its way into our sultry bedrooms.

I fell asleep to the sounds of occasional cars passing our corner, their headlights casting a spotlight that swept around my ceiling. On summer nights when the windows were open the room was filled with the sound of water cascading over the dam in the park just down the hill. In winter the wind rattled my windowpanes, and the branches of the huge maple trees in the yard made patterns on the dotted Swiss curtains in my windows, but I was safe inside.

...

I slept in that youth bed until my eighth year. The August before third grade I contracted polio. I was too young to realize the seriousness of the illness, but I'm sure it was a great worry to my family. Our pastor's family, just across the street from us, had lost a nine-year-old son to polio a few years earlier. After I had spent feverish day lying on the couch complaining of a stiff neck, my parents called the local doctor. That happened to be my cousin, Jack Lenton, newly graduated from medical school; he was filling in for Dr. Risser who was enjoying a well-deserved vacation.

I was in isolation at St. Mary's Hospital in Rochester for ten days. During that time my mother sent daily notes to me reminding me "to be a good girl, mind the nurses, and eat my meals." My bed was next to the window and at night my eyes were drawn to the lighted statue of an angel near the roofline. Two teenage girls shared the very tiny hospital room. One of them became paralyzed in her legs.

When I returned home to my room, it held an adult-sized twin bed with spindle head and footboards. On the pillow was a sign (done in my dad's handwriting) that read "Welcome Home, Maggie." The bed was tucked into the corner just like Margaret's bed had been situated, a cozy niche with a handy wall lamp that you could turn off after you were in the bed. The streetlight on the corner cast a dim light through the double curtained windows.

•••

Following their marriage my parents moved to Kasson, Minnesota, and two years later, my sister Wendy Ann, was born.

I never lived in Kasson, but I feel as though I did. The stories that were told about those years made it very real, and friendships that were formed there lasted many decades. Those were the war years, but my dad was exempt from service as he was involved in agribusiness and was needed on the home front.

Not too long ago, in a telephone conversation with Wendy, she told me that while cleaning a storage area, she had come across her baby book.

"I was baptized at home," she told me, "and I never knew that Margaret was one of my sponsors." The other sponsor was Mother's friend Lucy.

"Why do you think I was baptized at home?" she asked. "Do you think it was because Margaret was a Catholic and it was a Lutheran baptism? It was only the pastor, Mother, Dad, Margaret and Lucy (and probably Lucy's husband, Art)."

That left me wondering how my very Lutheran grandmother (Dad's mother) felt about being excluded. Did she ever know that Margaret was Mother's mother?

...

In March of 1946, my very pregnant mother, my dad and my sister left their life in Kasson for a new one in Stewartville. The story goes that my mother's labor was brought on by a bumpy five-mile ride over gravel country roads so that my sister could deliver a May basket to our Grandma Aletta. The next day, May 2, 1946, I arrived at Saint Mary's Hospital in Rochester, Minnesota. A distant cousin of my dad's, the former Marian Lenton, also delivered a girl that day, but luckily there were no mix-ups and I went home with the current Marion Lenton.

I left the hospital without a name. My birth certificate read: "Baby Girl Lenton." My parents had anticipated that their second child would be a boy and had chosen the name "Thomas Edward" (a name that Wendy would one day bestow on her second son). But sometime before I was baptized in June, I was given the name Margaret Jean – Margaret, after my "Aunt" Margaret.

Wendy, who was six when I was born, has told me that she had no warning that a new baby was coming into the house, and she was not pleased to share her space with a new family member!

I was baptized in July 1946, at Zion Lutheran Church in Stewartville. My sponsors were my Grandma Aletta and her husband, Fred, and my "Uncle" Matt and "Aunt" Charlotte.

...

The house I was brought to was to be my home for the next nineteen years. There were no street names in Stewartville, a town of about 1,000 in 1946, so my parent's new home was probably still referred to as the "Chandler" house. It was a square, Craftsman-style house that stood on a slight hill a block away from the park and Lake Florence. Dr. Hagen, a local dentist, who eventually became our next-door neighbor, lent my dad the money to make a down payment.

Wendy tells me that, as a baby, I slept in a crib in my parents' room, and that because I was sickly there were several trips to the hospital in Rochester during my infancy.

One of my earliest memories is of sitting under the round dining room table, snuggled in a little niche between two of the massive feet that came out from the main support, and playing with my "Audrey" doll. My mother was running the vacuum cleaner around the table, but I was safe and hidden behind the long lacy tablecloth that let in slits of sunlight.

...

The story about Margaret that Wendy and I had uncovered became the topic of nearly every conversation we had during the following year.

Several decades earlier my Aunt Mary (my dad's sister-in-law) who lived in California had come to visit the Minnesota relatives and had brought along something that truly interested me: some family history. She had dabbled in genealogy, and presented us with a family tree for the Lenton side of the family, as well as, photos of my grandfather, Robert, and his father, Charles. I was hooked!

This was probably in the late '60s, long before personal computers and the Internet, so Mary told me how to obtain birth and death records at county offices and how to use the archives of the Mormon Church.

For several years I submitted request after request and waited anxiously for return mail that might bring bits of information to add to the family trees I was tracing.

...

A few days after Mother's funeral, Dad went to Preston to get copies of her birth certificate. He never showed them to me, nor, at the time, did I ask to see them. He did reveal, though, that she was a year older than he had thought. She probably hadn't seen the birth certificate either, and was going by the incorrect date noted on her baptismal certificate, or maybe she didn't want Dad to know that she was really five years his senior. I feel certain she didn't hide her family secret from him. He didn't appear to be shocked by the birth certificate.

...

After discovering Mother's parentage, I began to make trips to Minnesota History Center a short distance from my home. I spent hours in the resource center there scanning rolls of microfiche copies of the Lanesboro newspapers, taking notes on any information pertaining to the Dent and Quarstad families. Through the social columns, I was able to track many of their activities, developing a timeline: Margaret was working as a nurse in several locations; Oscar (Mother's biological father), worked for the railroad, was a star player on the local baseball team, and then enlisted in the service; Margaret's father, Milton, became a cigar maker and on numerous occasions, "visited his family," which inferred that he didn't live with them.

···

My mother saved greeting cards when I was a child, and I still have many baby and birthday cards that were given to me during those years. Tucked in with my baby book are a congratulatory card from "Aunt Margaret" and a florist's card that reads *"Love Margaret – Wadena"* (she was working at Fair Oaks Lodge Sanitorium in

Wadena, Minnesota). Also saved were a first
birthday card, a get-well card, and another birthday
card with a slip of paper inside that said "*A gift
later when I get to Rochester.*" Margaret's
handwriting lacked loops, as did my mother's and
now mine.

My mother noted in my baby book that among
other gifts received were a nightgown, a sun suit,
and $10 (equivalent to $117 today) from Margaret.

...

The little knife with the ivory handle that sat on
Margaret's bedside table had always intrigued me.

What child isn't intrigued by a knife, especially
one like this, sheathed in an ivory case that had the
worn carving of an animal, perhaps a caribou or a
reindeer pulling what appeared to be a sleigh. A
piece of leather skirted the top of the case, and
attached to the leather was a short chain with a
hook at the end, probably for hooking the knife
unto a belt or through a buttonhole. The knife
blade was about two inches long and curved to a
very sharp point. On the bone handle of the knife

was another carving, again the head of a reindeer or caribou.

Margaret let me hold the knife occasionally, always with a warning to be careful.

After she died, the knife sat for years on one of the bookcases that flanked the fireplace in the house where I grew up. Fifteen years after Margaret's death, my parents built a new home and the knife again sat on the edge of a bookshelf, next to Margaret's books.

I don't remember the exact day that the knife came into my possession, but it probably was on a weekend visit home after my mother had died. Dad had remarried, and his wife, Fran, was always very gracious and told my sister and me to feel free to take anything in the house that held meaning for us.

Anyway, the knife came to live with me and it moved from house to house and country to country as my family towed its possessions in pursuit of my husband's career.

Once while I was thumbing through a country-style decorating magazine, an article about collectible Norwegian knives caught my eye.

There were pictures of knives that looked very similar to the knife I had.

So it came from Norway? How interesting! I filed that little tidbit in my mind, thinking that it might be fun to learn more about the possible value of the little knife

It was fate that revealed the value of the knife to me - fate that led Wendy and me into the museum's genealogy reference room.

The little knife that was nearly forgotten on my bookcase now intrigued me more than ever.

After all, Margaret had said "It belonged to a man who was in a war."

...

Another summer when Wendy came for a visit, we again went to Lanesboro, this time to Bethlehem Lutheran Church where we asked the church secretary to see the baptismal records from 1909 or 1910. There was Mother's baptism duly recorded: both parents listed and a Norwegian word heading one column. We asked what the word meant, and the secretary softly replied *'illegitimate."* Other Norwegian words on the certificate were later translated to me to mean "unofficial home baptism."

•••

Wendy and I had decided that we would like to speak with our "cousin," Carmen (Charlotte's daughter), to see if she knew anything about our family history. We knew that she was in declining health and weren't sure where she was, so shortly before Wendy's visit I was about to call her daughter, Becky, when a letter from Becky arrived informing me that her mother was in a care center.

We found Carmen in a Twin Cities area care center, and she, too, told us that she knew the story, but it wasn't talked about "because it wasn't anybody's business."

Shortly after our visit, I wrote this letter to Carmen's daughter Becky:

Dear Becky,

It is uncanny that your letter arrived when it did. Wendy was just here for a visit. She arrived on a Friday, and Saturday morning we discussed going to visit your mom. I said I'd have to call you to get the details about where she was, but when I got the mail a few minutes later, there was your letter!

Anyway, we went to visit her that Sunday. She looks great and seems in good spirits. We had a good visit about past times, but she was confused about Mom and Dad being gone. It must be very frustrating for all you girls...

Anyway, back to our family - Wendy and I discovered some interesting family history quite by accident last summer: that our mother was actually the daughter of Margaret Dent and not a sister to her, Clarence, Elvina, Agatha and your grandmother! She was born out of wedlock and raised by Milton and Carrie Dent as their daughter, not as their granddaughter. Maybe you knew that. We have verified it by birth and baptismal records and through conversations with Geraldine and your mother. We seem to be the only ones who didn't know it! It all makes sense now - why Mother didn't look like the rest of the Dent family, why Margaret spent the last three years of her life living with us, why your grandmother and the rest of the family always

talked fondly about our mother as "little Marion,"
and why I am named "Margaret."

To say that we were shocked is putting it
mildly! We felt really cheated that we hadn't
known that Margaret was our grandmother. We
know the name of Mother's father, have seen his
picture and researched much about his family. We
haven't attempted to locate any relatives on that
side though - don't know if we will.

I've become very intrigued with the Dent family
history. Did you find any photos of Margaret or of
Carrie and Milton? I would love to make some
copies if you have any.

Let's stay in touch and hopefully get everyone
together sometime soon.

Peggy

...

Still trying to unravel the puzzle, I called
Elvina's daughter, Mildred. She, too, knew the
story. Eleven years older than Mother, Mildred
said she was probably eighteen or twenty when she
was told that Mother was Margaret's child. She

did know, however, that when her parents were first married, that Mother had lived with them for a time.

"Margaret was like a stranger to me," she said. "She was hard to get close to. I always wondered if she was the daughter of Milton. She looked so different from the rest of the family. She had dark hair and none of the freckled skin like her siblings."

She told me that Milton and Carrie had led separate lives. Carrie had a restaurant in Preston, and her daughter, Agatha, lived with her and worked as a bookkeeper when Mother was in high school.

She remembered Margaret visiting once in a while bringing gifts for Mother and sometimes, for her, too, and her sister Geraldine.

I had one more conversation with Mildred and she recalled that on Sundays, Milton would sometimes walk from Lanesboro to her parents' farm, and she remembered" the sight of Grandpa coming up the hill, always dressed in a brown suit and a hat."

Mildred died shortly after sharing that conversation and another source of memory was gone.

...

Only a month after sending my letter to Becky, she called to say her mother had passed away at age 73.

On a brilliant autumn day, I made the drive from Hudson to Rochester to attend Carmen's funeral at Zumbro Lutheran Church. Becky was the first relative I encountered there.

"We're not as closely related as we thought, are we?" I said.

"No," she replied, "but I have some letters that I need to give to you. They came from my grandmother's attic."

I felt a great sense of loss at Carmen's funeral. She and her sister, Bobby (Vera Mae), Charlotte's daughters, and Geraldine and Mildred, Elvina's daughters (who we had considered cousins), had always been interested in Wendy and me, even though they were a generation older, and now, all of them were gone.

Chapter 4

Later that fall, Don and I went to Northfield to the home of Becky and her husband, Tony, both economics professors at St. Olaf College. Ready for me was a stack of yellowed envelopes and pieces of correspondence -tied together with a red cord. It contained letters, receipts and other correspondence from a half dozen family members, addressed to many different locations, spilling out stories concerning my mother's parentage. How did they all end up in Becky's grandmother's (my "Aunt" Charlotte's) attic and why were they saved?

The bundle of yellowed papers weighed heavily on me. There was a story to uncover and it was in my hands.

...

Most telling of all was a letter to Margaret's father from Dr. Arthur B. Ancker of the City and County Hospital in St. Paul, Minnesota.

It read:

Mar. 13, 1909

Mr. Milton J. Dent
    Lanesboro, Filmore, Co. Minn.

Dear Sir:

The day before yesterday, your daughter Margaret called at the hospital presenting a letter from one of the Sisters at St. Mary's Hospital, Rochester, Minn. asking that she be admitted and cared for at this hospital.

Regretfully as I do it, it is still to my mind necessary that I should advise you of the fact that your daughter is in a delicate condition and according to her story will be confined sometime in August.

She being almost without means – certainly without sufficient to purchase her return ticket to Lanesboro, we have temporarily cared for her, though if she is to remain with us until she is confined, arrangements will have to be made to meet her expenses. She being a non-resident of this county, if she is to become a public charge, we

*will have to apply to the public authorities of
Filmore County. We trust, however, that such a
step will not be necessary and that you will
arrange either to take her home or to take care of
her account while here. I trust you will feel that
the poor child has been unfortunate and should be
an object of sympathy and not of condemnation.
We will agree to take care of her at the rate of one
dollar ($1.00) per day.*

Please let us hear from you.
Yours truly,
Arthur B. Ancker
Supt.

At the bottom of the letter, written in pencil is this
notation:
*(Bearer of this letter is Wife of Milton J. Dent,
Lanesboro).*

...

    To whom did Carrie bear this letter? Had she
opened the letter because she suspected what the
content concerned? Or had Milton given her the
letter?

Earlier letters and bills from 1892 and 1893 (also in the bundle), led me to imagine that Milton and Carrie's marriage got off to a shaky start. During their first years together they lived in Rushford, Minnesota, where they ran a restaurant and bakery. According to two bills from a wholesale grocer in La Crosse, Milton owed money, but Carrie had taken charge of the business and was trying to pay off the bills.   In 1892, just two years into their marriage, Carrie sent this letter (found among the papers tied with red cord) to J.J. Hogan, Wholesale Grocer in La Crosse:

"The bill my husband owes you is $178 as near as I figure it. I offered you 20 per cent in full last winter. You said you would take it. I now send on $35.40. It is all I can do as the winter and spring are awful – no trade or show of future trades . I will reconsider you in my orders in the future as in the past and trust you will never loan another penny here. See receipt in full."

A subsequent letter from J.J. Hogan is addressed to C. G .Chapman (an attorney) in Lanesboro, explaining what Carrie owes on account and ending *"Let me know if you make her understand the matter."*

A receipt for the $35.40 also was among the pack of papers.

A year later, in 1893, J.J. Hogan, Wholesale Grocer, sent this memo to Chapman:

"The unpaid portion of M.J. Dent is for him, not Mrs. Dent. I do understand she claims a settlement for the full account. I gave this agency, Bankers & Merchants, a number of old accounts, this among them. If she has any receipts in full for this unpaid portion of course I would not expect anything more. Please inform me just how the matter stands."

Then, in correspondence with the letterhead "M.J. Dent, Restaurant and Bakery, Confectionery, Fruits, etc," Milton wrote to Chapman:

Enclosed you will please find a receipt in full and a letter from J.J. Hogan stating that he will accept 20 per cent on account, which, of course, we have done....

I did not think it necessary to send you all the old bills and receipts, statements and so forth, so I send you his letter and receipt in full."

Hogan follows with a letter acknowledging the settlement writing: *"I will notify the collection agency to discontinue the claim."*

A letter from Chapman, dated a few days later, informs M.J. Dent and wife *"we guess all is well."*

...

A few years later, according to the 1900 census, Milton and Carrie and four children were residing in Lanesboro and had three boarders living with them. Carrie was probably earning money cooking and doing laundry for those three men.

...

In another revealing letter, one of Milton's siblings (the signature was missing, but it presumably was a sister) wrote to him from Chicago in 1902. On letterhead stationery from the Briggs House Hotel, the writer says she has just arrived from Milwaukee and is on her way to Omaha.

The letter says:

"You must write me how things turn out – I did all I could for you while out your way and am going to do all I can for you all the time, only you must not get mad at me for anything I say or write to you.

I don't wonder you get discouraged, that is natural, but it only puts things back. Take the bull by the horns and make up your mind that you will succeed, and succeed you will if you will only conform to the thoughts of other people, let them boss. 'taint half so much trouble to be bossed as it is to boss someone else, and what do you care, all you want is some way of making an honest living. You let the other fellow do the bossing and fussing and you do the mechanical part of it. You don't care how he wants it done. I want to help you all I can. Take your violin with you wherever you go, it may lead to a thousand avenues and is very elevating. Clint said something about you painting his house for him and asked how much you got a day. I told him I thought $1.50 per day, of course that was in Lanesboro where you did not have to

*pay board, not in La Crosse where you would have
to pay board, don't you see.*

*You have a nice family and one of the very best
wives that ever lived. Now all will be well and
come around right in time if you can only make up
your mind to take people as they are as they take
you as you are. All this figuring and planning is
more help to you than actual money, which I could
not give even if I wished to. Put yourself in the
way for steady employment for this winter, so you
will not have it so hard another winter. Clint said
perhaps there might be an opening somewhere for
the running of a stationary engine. If you could
get something like that, it would pay you better
than the streetcar service, but if you go in the
streetcar service, seems to me the motorman's
place would be a much better place for you than
conductor. Making change in a hurry in a
crowded car would be very confusing, I should
think, and I'm afraid you'd be wanting to put
somebody off ere long, cause they would not do as
you thought they should, and then, too, if you
would cuss anybody you would be reported and
there would be some more bad language and no
end of trouble.*

Say Honey, don't get tired reading this. I'm helping you all the time. You must write me just as soon as anything happens. But be sure now and take your violin with you, if you only go to La Crosse for a day or so. Clint's boys will enjoy it immensely. Just fix up a little and brush yourself to the front a little and everybody will show you a welcome if you hide the tobacco and cuss words, but you must look nice and smile a little like other folks.

Yours with love to all"

...

A this stage of his life, Milton had been married twelve years and was the father of Margaret, 11, Clarence, 7, Agatha and Elvina, 4, and Charlotte, 6 months. Was he making enough to support his family?

An out-of-focus photo shows Milton, his hands in his pockets, wearing a suit, vest, white shirt, tie and hat, accompanied by Margaret and her brother Clarence. Clarence is wearing a white shirt and overalls, Margaret a drop-waist long plaid dress.

Barely visible are the outlines of wire glasses on her face.

•••

Also among the papers tied with red cord was a very small scrap of paper dated "Portage, Feb. 9, 1905" which read:

"Dear Milton,

Warring (his brother) *is very ill of Pleuro pneumonia. Was taken sick on Sunday evening and we fear will not live to see another Sunday evening –*

Mother –

M. Dent"

Milton's brother Warring (next youngest in the family) did die at age 42 in 1905. Whether Milton made it to Portage to see him before he died is not known.

•••

It is documented that within a year of Mother's birth, in 1909, Milton and Carrie would be maintaining separate households. I can only speculate that Margaret's pregnancy had caused a deeper chasm in their troubled marriage.

There is no record of Margaret ever graduating from high school, and in March 1909, when Dr. Anker wrote the letter, she would have been only 17, approaching her next birthday in May. Yet, she was working (probably in a housekeeping position) at St. Mary's Hospital in Rochester. Did she drop out of school because of the family's financial needs or had she told her mother of her pregnancy and it was hoped that it could be covered up by sending her to the sisters in Rochester? Did the father of her child know of her pregnancy?

The letter informs Milton that his "daughter is in a delicate condition" – something he already knew as later documented in one of the letters that came tied with red cord.

...

I once took a friend to have a procedure done at Regions Hospital in St. Paul. While I was waiting for her, I wandered the halls and read the history of the hospital told in words and pictures along the walls. City and County Hospital was the predecessor of Regions Hospital and there was a lengthy homage to Dr. Anker who served the hospital for more than forty years . A photograph reveals a man with a receding hairline, a bowl of heavy hair along the back of his head, bushy eyebrows and a prominent nose, authoritative, yet kindly looking. It was probably part of his job to write many letters similar to the one concerning Margaret.

•••

I don't know if Margaret came home immediately after Dr. Anker's letter, but I do know that Mother was born (presumably at home) in Lanesboro August 2, 1909.

How did Oscar's parents react to their oldest son fathering a child? Did they know?

•••

There is so much I don't know, but from the opinion I formed of Milton after reading some later letters, I would guess that learning his unmarried daughter was pregnant would have greatly angered him. Lanesboro was a town of less than 1,000 in 1909 where gossip was likely to pass quickly.

The plan hadn't worked the way it was intended to work.

After months of worry, 17-year-oldMargaret had finally confided to her mother that she was pregnant. The two had only talked about it in hushed tones or when Milton was out of the house, because both women knew it would send him into a rage.

But it couldn't be hidden much longer.

"I think the thing for you to do is to leave high school and get a job as a nurse's aide in Rochester," counseled Carrie. "The Catholic sisters there will care for you, and you can give the baby up for adoption. No one in town will have to know about it."

Margaret was thoroughly shamed. How had she allowed this to happen? There was no promise of love or marriage, and now she was alone with her problem.

But her mother's advice seemed the best way out.

Telling her friends that she needed to earn some money, she said her good-byes and left in her senior year of high school.

The letters among those tied with red cord indicate that it had to have been tense in the Dent household. Milton showed no compassion (in one later virulent letter to her father, Margaret referred to the day "you made me sign your deceitful papers, agreeing to leave"). I would surmise that Carrie's mother's heart filled her with compassion.

...

Mother's birth could not have gone unnoticed in Lanesboro. Surely everyone knew Margaret was her mother. Margaret's siblings were sixteen, thirteen and eight - did they not talk about the new baby in their household?

Mother was passed off as one of the Dent children, but Milton would have been 47, and Carrie, 48, when she was born. In later years, didn't people question how she could have had such old parents?

Also tied with the red cord were two notes from Mother's biological father, "Mike" (Oscar) Quarstad, to Margaret's father, Milton, concerning money he owed Milton and a bank receipt showing that in December of 1909 he either deposited or agreed to deposit a total of $375 (the equivalent of $9,400 in today's money market) in an account for Milton with the notation *"Any money received on note to be delivered to Margaret Dent and Marion Dent on equal shares. Marion Dent's share to be deposited in bank until she becomes of age."*

There, in black and white, was more proof that Oscar was my mother's father and also that he took financial responsibility for her. It is interesting that he signed his name "Mike," to me an indication that he was breaking away from his Norwegian heritage with a more Americanized name. Did Oscar voluntarily agree to make support payments or had Milton confronted him?

...

The 1910 census taken in April reveals that, eight months after giving birth, Margaret was again at St. Mary's Hospital in Rochester. A newspaper item notes that by July she was employed at Lutheran Hospital in La Crosse.

Marion was left in the care of her grandmother.

That same 1910 census report (the one that had shocked Wendy and me), lists Carrie as head of the household, living in Lanesboro with children Clarence, Elvina & Agatha, and Charlotte, and granddaughter, Marion. Milton had evidently moved out by then. Carrie is noted as being the employer in a restaurant.

Oscar, 22, is still listed as a member of his parents' household in the 1910 census, along with his younger siblings, Edwin, Agnes, Leonard and Helen.

...

The Lanesboro Leader of May 14, 1910 reported:

"The rooms vacated by J.G. French in the Journal building are now occupied by M.J. Dent, the cigar maker. M.J. has come down a peg on location but says "Royal Honor" cigars will contain the same amount of good, clean smoke as before and that sure is enough for 5 cents."

On the back of one of his statement forms that proclaim "M.J. Dent, Manufacturer of High-Grade Cigars," Milton had recorded his rent payments of

$4 a month, the first payment made on the day of Margaret's nineteenth birthday.

...

    I knew very little about Mother's early years. There were a few photos of the woman she called "mother," Carrie Dent, and only two fuzzy pictures of her "father," Milton Dent. They both died years before I was born. All she had ever told me was that Milton had been a violin teacher, and, that at one time, Carrie had had a restaurant.

    The one blurred photograph I have of my mother with Milton shows her standing by his side, while he is seated in a leather chair. His leg is crossed in a casual manner, and he is holding a violin in one hand, the bow in the other. In the background against the floral wallpaper is a pennant with the words "Fergus Falls" on it. I would surmise it was a gift from Margaret (who was working at a state institution there) and that the photo was probably taken in Carrie's house. Knowing what I now know, I doubt that Margaret would have given such a pennant to Milton.

Chapter 5

From later records I know that Milton gave violin lessons, and his death certificate notes that his profession was a "musician" for more than 60 years. Was there music in their home? Did he play for functions? I don't know.

My mother loved music. She played the piano well, mentioned that she had had a few violin lessons, loved to sing, and chose a career as an elementary school music teacher.

I have vivid memories of her singing to Wendy and me before bed or as we rode in the car, especially our favorite songs "Baby's Boat's a Silver Moon" and "My Mommy Told Me."

Her strong soprano voice heard above all others in church almost embarrassed me. When I was young she often performed in duets and trios at services. I sang in a children's choir at church and then didn't participate in vocal music until my senior year in high school. That year I also joined the church choir and Mother and I faithfully went to practice once a week and then sang on Sundays.

Among the papers tied with red cord was this scrap of paper dated September 20, 1910, from Carrie addressed to M J Dent, who was by then living in Fountain, Minnesota.

It reads:

M J Dent

I received your letter with a chick of five dollars for Marion that you had received from M quarstad to aply on his note.

You return that note to the Bank at once or it shall be trouble. I will not Put one cent of that money in the Bank on till you return the note.

I shall not take any more of your deceiving Worke at all.

Mrs M J Dent

The note clearly accuses Milton of absconding with money that was meant for my mother I have no way of knowing if he was supporting his family while he lived apart or if he was hard up for money, but it seems a despicable thing to do, to take money meant for your granddaughter.

Items from the Lanesboro newspaper of 1912, report that Margaret, referred to as a nurse at St. Mary's Hospital in Rochester, had been home on a visit in January. St. Mary's opened a two-year nurses' training school in 1906. Was Margaret taking some training courses?

According to a 1998 *Newsweek* article that commemorated 100 years of nursing, student nurses in the early 1900s typically worked 10-12-hour shifts, training in programs that were described as "rigorous and exhausting." A new student began working primarily as a maid, doing household chores of dusting, scrubbing walls and furniture and washing dishes.

...

In March of that year Milton traveled to Preston and Wykoff looking for sites for his cigar business.

The newspaper noted in May that Margaret was ill in Rochester with scarlet fever and that her mother had traveled to Rochester to be with her.

The June 1, 1912, edition of *The Lanesboro Leader* included this item:

"Lanesboro is now without a cigar maker. M.J. Dent who has been in business here for the last

*four years closed shop last week and on
Wednesday took leave for Caledonia where he has
rented a building and will open a cigar factory at
once. Mr. Dent is a good cigar maker, quiet and
attentive to business, and his friends here hope
that his venture will be both pleasant and
profitable."*

In Caledonia Milton produced cigars with the
labels "Royal Honor," "Three Oak," "Mild &
Rich," and "Full Value." He now lived
approximately twenty-five miles from his family.

...

Meanwhile, Carrie, nearing fifty, was running a
restaurant and holding the family together. Mother
would have turned three that year, and I imagine
that the older girls in the family were caring for her
- the twins would have been nearly thirteen.

Did Oscar or members of his family stare at the
dark-eyed little girl with the long black locks when
they certainly encountered her in their small town?
There is no evidence that Oscar's parents or
siblings had knowledge of the daughter he had
fathered. However, in one of Margaret's letters to

her father she chides him for speaking openly about her as his "loose" daughter. Didn't that talk spread throughout the tiny community?

...

Many professional photos of Mother during her girlhood years remain. I assume that Margaret must have paid for them, as I doubt that Carrie made enough money in her restaurant to pay for such frivolous extras. Milton, too, had to have been earning a meager income making cigars and giving violin lessons, and both he and Carrie were maintaining separate living quarters.

In one professional photo, Mother is wearing a beautiful wool coat trimmed with fur and is holding a fashionable fur muff.

Marion Dent

According to the newspaper, Milton spent Christmas Day 1912 with his family, evidence that he had not completely abandoned them, but there must have been tension between him and Carrie.

...

During Mother's childhood years, Margaret, continued to work in hospitals or state institutions.

In 1914, when Mother was five, Margaret became employed at a state institution in Fergus Falls, Minnesota.

Curious to know more about this institution, I traveled to Fergus Falls. It's impossible to miss the facility as it commands an imposing site on a hill above the city. At a county museum I was presented with several boxes of papers and pictures that took me into the life of the Fergus Falls State Hospital. Completed in 1899, the hospital was designed to house the insane, the epileptic, and the "lovesick" – some 300 patients. During the time Margaret worked at the facility there were 2,000 patients and 250 employees. Treatment used would today be termed "inhumane"- patients' heads were shaved, they were chained, and some were made to wear masks to prevent biting. Rooms were locked at 8 p.m. and morning call was at 5 a.m. Hydrotherapy consisted of being wrapped in wet sheets and heavy woolen blankets that were securely pinned, having an ice pack on the head and a hot water bottle on the feet. Patients also were immersed in continuous flow tubs of blood-temperature water for long periods of time.

In sharp contrast to the treatment methods, the blocks-long, horseshoe-shaped hospital was built in the Kirkbride style, reflecting a philosophy promoted by Dr. Thomas Kirkbride who wanted to conceive ideal sanctuaries for the mentally ill by creating light-filled institutions akin to resort hotels.

On-line pictures now show an interior of peeling paint, but still visible are beautiful tiled-floor hallways, stairways with ornate railings, and hall areas with rows of windows.

How did Margaret react to this workplace? Did she feel threatened? She stayed at Fergus Falls for several years, most likely living in the on-campus nurses' home. The facility had a training school for nurses and it is possible that Margaret took some training there.

...

The room is sparsely furnished- a chair, a dresser, and a night stand for each of the ten beds, most likely like every other state nurses' dormitories.

Even the clothes in Margaret's dresser are sparse: a couple of white uniforms, white slips, white stockings, white shoes, and starched white hats. Only two "civilian" dresses and a few accessories are needed as she is rarely off duty.

The common area of the dormitory, however, is quite comfortable. Decorated in Craftsman style, the main gathering room features a brick fireplace, a piano, chairs, benches and table, round globe ceiling lights and Oriental rugs on the floor – a welcome respite from the clamor of the wards.

The work is hard, the rules strict, and the hours long. Margaret often has to wrestle a patient to get that patient to submit to treatment or to eat or to go to bed. Only 23, she is strong, but it is demanding work often filled with endless cleaning duties. Sleep comes easily at the end of the day – too easily. There is little time to think of Marion, of home, of her family.

How she wishes she could be the one to hold Marion, to caress her dark hair, to sing her to sleep. But she'd better not wish too hard or she may let something slip. What if others found out her secret?

She pens the note on the back of the postcard picture of herself with her friend: "With Love to Little Mija from…"and then uses the black ink to blot out the word "Mother."

Margaret Dent

Milton visited his family in the spring of 1914, and *Levang's Weekly* of Lanesboro reported in an April edition: "M J Dent, the hustling cigar manufacturer of Caledonia, spent Easter with his family here in Lanesboro. He expressed himself as very well satisfied with business conditions in spite of the fact that the county option election wiped the saloons out of Caledonia."

Any mention of Milton in newspapers refers to him as "M J," evidently the moniker he used. I find it ironic that my initials also are M. J. and so are those of a granddaughter.

In late August of 1916, Milton again visited Lanesboro and the September 7 edition of *LeVang's* reported: "M.J. Dent, the Lanesboro man who manufactures cigars at Caledonia, is quite a frequent visitor at his home here. While here last week, he made arrangements with Mr. C. A. Knatterud (a local druggist) to handle his cigars. He has two brands on the market, both five-cent cigars, and both strictly long filters and made of the best stock. Next time you buy a cigar at the drug store, better call for a "Cuban Club" or a "Mild and Rich.""

Two letters from Oscar to Milton survive from 1916.

On September 15, Oscar wrote:

Mr. M.J. Dent:

Dear Sir:

Am sending you $5 five dollars by express money order for which please give me credit and receipt. You said it would be satisfactory if I paid u $5 Every 2 weeks. I shall be glad to do so, and am going to ask you if it would make any difference to you if I got married. I think if I got married I could save more money and pay you up sooner. I hope Mr. Dent that this will be satisfactory and that you will ans. at once - I am
Yours Very Truly

Mike Quarstad
Gen. Del. Austin, Minn.

A receipt among the papers records that on September 8, 1916 (a week prior to Oscar's note) Milton (who now lived in Caladonia) paid five dollars to Margaret. Two days later, she answered with this scathing letter:

Dear Father-

Rec'd your letter, also money order.

Was glad to hear, -But- please send <u>Mother </u>the money its not mine - its Marion's and Ma is the one who is caring for her.

I sent her the five you sent me. - I dont want it. Put it in the bank where it <u>belongs</u>.

"I" havent the heart to wilfully take what by <u>law</u> belongs to my child.

She is robed of a birth right simply to satisfy someone else. But it is injustice to take what can clothe & feed an unfortunate, and I think if you reason for a minute or two you'll see the difference.

For tempers sake you have ruined my childs life as well as my own.

I'm only one of the million who was led astray - and I dont see why I couldn't have been treated accordingly. The idea a father who pretends he is doing it for the best to her face - Behind her back darkens her whole path. Is that honorable is it justice.

I thought you said that note was signed over to me and in Habberstads bank for collect. Father when you are so false? How can you expect us to respect you - leaving love out intirly?

You've had trouble with your own Sis & Bro - uncle & cousins and so on - we are not to blame for that you married (?) parted you in your first family trouble surely not my mother nor us children. I've never known a Father who dislike his wife & children so they would speak or who would be jealous of a childs love for its Mother. Your the odd man I'm afraid instead as an other father would do, keep his misfortunes his family troubles and his childrens quiet for a gossipers sake you make it publicaly known. Because your Boss. Still its awfull when we dont honor, write & fall all over you in love - which we all would if we had any grounds to put it to -
M-

This is the first of Margaret's many angry letters that came tied with the red cord. Following correspondence further documents her fractured relationship with her father.

Just a few months later, on December 5, Oscar wrote this letter:

Mr. M.J. Dent:
Dear Sir:
I must write u a few lines in regard to what I owe u. I got hurt the 13th of Oct. and didn't make a trip on the road until the 1st of Dec. so you see that I've been up against it. But just as soon as my pay starts again I shall do all that I can to keep my payments up as I would like very much to get squared up with you. Hoping you will be satisfied for the time being. I am
Yours Truly

Mike Quarstad

Was Milton making frequent trips to Lanesboro to pick up the checks from Oscar? Evidently Oscar was making payments directly to him.

In spite of conflict with Carrie and Margaret, it appears that Milton did maintain contact with his family in Lanesboro. Charlotte recalled taking a picture of him and Marion with a Brownie camera that she had received for Christmas.

They stare intently at the camera in the now blurred photograph that I have of my mother with Milton. It is Christmas Day, and Milton is spending it with his family in the house where he no longer lives. He is seated in a leather chair, has his leg crossed in a casual manner, and he is holding a violin in one hand, the bow in the other. Dressed for the holiday, he has on a suit, a white shirt and tie, and some high topped shoes. Charlotte, age twelve, peers into her new box camera at the scene in front of her.

My mother's thick black hair is curled in ringlets that hang by her ears and her bangs are combed straight across her forehead. Four years old, she is wearing a dress with a dropped waist and what looks to be some high-topped shoes. She stands close to Milton, resting her arm upon the arm of the chair. Both of them look very

*serious as they hold their pose: Milton's
mustache conceals his lips.*

*The aroma of the Christmas dinner meatballs
mixes with the odor of the kerosene heater, and
the windows are steamed against the winter's
cold. Music had flowed through the house that
afternoon as Milton's violin sang to his family,
soothing their torn relationship. Marion loved
the music and, caught up in the holiday gaiety,
danced around the room.*

Milton and Marion

Through articles in the 1916 Lanesboro newspaper, I discovered that Norwegian services were still being held at the Lutheran church. In January, elementary students, Marion and Helen Quarstad (Oscar's sister, and Marion's aunt), were cited for not being absent or tardy. Did those two little girls who were in the same classroom play together? Was either of them aware of their relationship to each other?

Chapter 6

In April of 1917, immediately after the U.S. declaration of war, Oscar enlisted in the service and reported to Camp Cody, New Mexico, to train as a member of the Coast Guard.

A month later, in May 1917, Margaret received her nursing degree from Mt. Pleasant (Iowa) State Hospital Training School for Nurses. There are no records to indicate how long she was at this school or how lengthy the training was. Did she receive credit for all her prior years of nursing experience? It is noteworthy that in a time when not many women worked outside the home, she achieved a degree and worked to support herself and her child.

Mother was nearing her eighth birthday by this time. Her mother was in Iowa, her father in the service, and she was in her grandmother's care, probably being looked after by Charlotte who was sixteen.

Charlotte and Marion, an early photograph

...

While home on leave in June 1917, (nine months after asking Milton if it would make any difference if he got married) Oscar married Cora Olson in Austin, Minnesota, and then returned to duty.

A few months later, in September, he was transferred to Presidio, California.

Early in 1918 Margaret returned to Mt. Pleasant to work in the state hospital there. Prior to that time, she had spent several weeks caring for her sister, Agatha, who had been ill at the home of a cousin near Lanesboro.

Returning from Florida one spring on an extended trip along the Mississippi River, I was at the wheel when I spied a road sign with an arrow pointing left to Mt. Pleasant. Without hesitating I put on the blinker and Don and I drove into the quaint town, complete with a large town square.

Early in the 20th century, Mt. Pleasant gained fame as a birthplace of feminism and liberalism: the P.E.O. sisterhood was founded there at Wesleyan College, and a hall in the downtown area had been the site of speeches given by Frederick Douglas and Sojourner Truth. A portion of the state institution where Margaret had worked remained, a short distance from town, - now used to house a mental health facility.

Built in 1861, the site was the oldest of Iowa's facilities serving persons affected with mental illnesses. Originally known as the Iowa Lunatic Asylum, the name was later changed to Iowa

Insane Asylum, Iowa Hospital for the Insane and, finally, Iowa Mental Health Institute.

Pictures show a facility also built in the Kirkbride style, a four-story central portion with three-story wings. The lobby featured a sweeping stairway; the patient rooms appeared sunny and bright . In 1871 the facility had 450 patients, but a fire in 1936 destroyed most of the buildings.

...

At the end of January 1918 Margaret wrote to her father at his Fountain, Minnesota, address.

Dad:-

Rec'd your letter - or rather letters- was glad to hear. Am well - hope this find you the same.

Rather cold her presume its the same in Minnesota. Have you seen Agatha - or haven't you been home?

Circumstances did not permit staying in Lanesboro any longer than I did or rather making any visits.

I hear from home occassionally.

*Further more a visit could not help - so thats
the reason I did not loiter around calling - possible
would of been of no interest as your way of seeing
life & mine are far apart.*

*You mention in your letter some day we
children will see our mistakes perhaps for respect
sake we may - but at the present not...*

*we got lots to thank you for - lots to remember
you for. The Days going to come you'll see your
mistakes (perhaps when its to late) as you
mentioned to me.*

*I've got lots to thank you for haven't I - robbing
my child of a wordly name. How can you face her
knowing that thru your threat & hateful dispotition
she has to face the whole world as she does. Your
a Father to be proud of - aren't you? remember
my life was wrecked by you ten years ago- and my
feeling for you in that respect are as fresh as the
Mon. of Nov. 1908 that you made me sign (agreen
to leave) your decitful papers, and my feeling shall
remain so.* (Mother was born August 2 the next
year, so Margaret could only have been two
months pregnant that November. Did Milton
know she was pregnant or was he angry that she
had been with Oscar?).

*You made me out in public to be indecent well -
alright - but how can such supposed upright man
as you sneak around watch for ever dollar that
might come in to my child thru her Father
(remember now I said her Father) and spend it
freely as you do or did.*

*What about the money you've drawn? Where is
it - Is it where an honest man puts it? Dont you
know your handling or living on fast womens
money - you classed me as such to your friend -
court & public.*

*How can you lower yourself - stain your clean
reputation if you ever had any.*

*Just a few reminders of your actions toward me
in my 26 years of life isnt enough is it.*

*How much more do I need as for the Xmas $. its
home save it to wipe the tears from Marions eyes
when she's old enough to realize her
circumstance...*

*here after dont waste paper pen or ink or even
your thought on me - for there like the bite of a
snake.*

*As for myself morally - I'm as clean in thoughts
& action as any human breathing, except for hate*

and as for what injury you can do either to me or any of the home folks with that tongue of yours…
Margret

Written in the margin is: *"Show this to whom you please if you still make it your business to make family affairs public."*

At the end of the letter, Charlotte, who found the letter in her attic, wrote *"Whew!"* and dated it 1976. *"I just now read this. How it got in my attic I don't know. Dad never spoke a harsh word to me."*

Why such an incriminating letter wasn't ever destroyed is hard to imagine, but it has survived, and the truth with it: Milton shamed Margaret and ordered her to leave home. What a chasm this must have created in his marriage.

While her nursing diploma spells her name as Margaret, the letter is signed "Margret."

…

Also among the letters tied with the red cord was a note on a small sheet of unlined tablet paper written in a child's scrawl.

Dated February 8, 1918, it read:

Dear daddy

How are you, I am fine. I wrote a letter before - but I tore it up because Agatha was finding all kinds of think about it. I am sending a picture of me. Well I'll have to close.

With love

Marion

I assume, that since it was found among Dent family letters, it was addressed to Milton who in 1918 was living in Fountain. After Margaret's hateful letter, it serves as a sweet reminder of eight-year-old Marion's love for her "father."

...

A January issue of the Lanesboro newspaper lists those who contributed to the rebuilding fund for Bethlehem Lutheran Church, which had been heavily damaged by fire. Among those contributing are members of the Dent, Ellingson (Carrie's family) and Quarstad families. In March of 1918, the rebuilt church was dedicated. Also noted in the paper in May is a Red Cross auction, with Carrie Dent and Wilhelmina Quarstad, Oscar's mother, among those who donated baked goods.

Obviously these two women came in contact often through the church and around town. Were they civil to one another? Did Wilhelmina ever inquire about Marion? Did she know about her?

...

In July 1918, word arrived that Margaret's brother, Clarence, had arrived in France where he would take part in battle.

Meanwhile, Oscar was training in California. Margaret remained at Mt. Pleasant State Hospital.

By October, Oscar had become a victim of the Spanish Flu.

Row upon row of cots covered the expansive floor of the armory building that had been pressed into service as a hospital ward. It wasn't for old men, but, rather, for young men too young to be facing death.

Through his bleary eyes, Oscar looked to the man on his right and then to the man on his left. A screen had been set up on his left while he had been sleeping, and he could no longer see his army mate, but he could hear his shallow breaths, his raspy cough, and the whispering voices surrounding him. He knew the end was near for Harry.

Oscar turned his back to the screen causing him to feel the intense aching in his body, the heaviness of his head. Only two days ago he had been out in the brilliant California sun, taking part in training exercises and now he was barely able to move. The Spanish Flu had drifted west to Camp Taliaferro, and he had watched as one man after another had fallen ill.

"Can I beat this?" he wondered. "Some men have walked away and I intend to be one of them. Does my wife know that I'm sick? Do my parents know?"

His thoughts carried him home to his small Midwest town. His wife was there with his newborn son that he had yet to see. His family was there on Coffee Street. And…the daughter

*he had fathered, who was now nine years old,
was there. Would he see them again?*

*As a member of the U.S. Army he had trained,
knowing that he probably would be sent overseas
to fight in the Great War, but now he lay on a cot,
on the home front battlefield, surrounded by
death and dying.*

He closed his eyes...

...

In mid-October, word reached Lanesboro that
Oscar Quarstad had died of the Spanish Flu. His
wife, Cora was left with a three-month-old son.

Was Carrie the first in the family to hear the
news? Did she feel pangs of sorrow when she
looked at Marion that day? Did she telephone or
write a letter to Margaret in Mt. Pleasant?

What was Milton's reaction? Was money his
only thought; did he feel any compassion, any
regrets? Was Marion aware of the community-
wide tribute to the "man who died in a war?"

Tribute to Oscar Quarstad

There is a gap in the family history from the time of Oscar's death in 1918 until the 1920 census. That census noted that Carrie Dent, 58, was married *(but was actually separated)* and the proprietor of a restaurant. Residing in her house were: Clarence, son, (home from the war), a farm laborer; Agatha, 21, daughter, teacher in public schools; Charlotte, 18, daughter; Marien, 10, _granddaughter_; Sophie Olson, 17, servant and restaurant worker, and John Gorman, 52, single, boarder, a carpenter. Carrie was once again evidently making ends meet by putting up two boarders.

Listed in another Lanesboro home was Milton Jerome Dent, 58, married, *(but separated)* homeowner, a cigar maker and proprietor of a cigar shop.

Oscar's parents, Odin and Minnie, were still living in Lanesboro with three children at home: Edwin, 21, Leonard, 15, and Helen, 11.

Oscar's widow, Cora, 20, also living in Lanesboro, is noted as a homemaker, residing with her 15-month-old son, Orval Lowell.

Soon after this census, Carrie and Marion moved to Preston, a short distance away. There, Carrie again, ran a restaurant. A January 1921edition of *The Preston Republican* includes the 1920 financial statement for Fillmore County: Receiving $9.75 for meals for jurors was Mrs. J.M. (?) Dent. Carrie evidently used her cooking skills to earn some extra money.

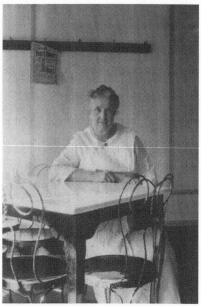

Carrie Dent

In April, 1921, Margaret wrote to her father from Yankton, S. D. where was she working in yet another state institution, Yankton State Hospital. Originally Dakota Hospital for the Insane, it also accommodated alcoholics and epileptics.

The post card says:

Dear Father:-

You welcomed letter as usual pleased to hear. Dont mention the Easter card - it was but a mere Rememberance.

Havent written to Marion yet - but- will soon. Had a letter from Elvina saying she was O.K.

(Elvina's daughter, Geraldine, had told me that Mother lived for a short time with Elvina and Gordon during their early marriage, probably to give Carrie a respite. Mother would have been 12 at that time).

Did you find out about the "violin" you spoke of sometime ago?

I am certain its not the violin that I use to have thats out to Johnson's.

Yet having sold it - I was no longer interested as to its wher about - still I felt pretty certain that

"Agatha" wouldent leave it out there she thot to much of it.

Space is use and so must close - Margret

Such a matter-of- fact letter - Margaret exchanging niceties with Milton three years after her scorching letter . And why is "Agatha" surrounded by quotation marks as if Margaret is belittling her name. And again, Margaret leaves the second "a" out of her name.

. . .

Margaret walked from the nurses' dormitory across the path that intersected the expansive manicured lawn of the state hospital. She observed the intense blueness of the sky and felt the warmth of the sun as she reached for her key to let herself into the first-floor ward where she would be on duty into the night.

Beds were arranged neatly in rows along the walls of the wards but bedclothes were in disarray on most of the beds. There was a constant clattering of metal dishes being dropped on the tile floor, the unmistakable odor of urine slightly masked by antiseptic cleanser, and the babbling

and frequent screams of patients some with serious mental illnesses, others wanting to escape their imprisonment.

She fingered some of the keys she wore on the chain around her waist. There were keys for every door, every cupboard. No patient was to be trusted.

Many would view her job as frightening, but she was used to this world sheltered from so many. Her work at St. Mary's in Rochester, at the Red Wing hospital, and at Gunderson Hospital in La Crosse had mainly involved tidying patient rooms, changing beds, mopping floors. But at Fergus Falls and Mt. Pleasant she found herself surrounded by patients with the potential to be violent. She tried to remain calm, to be friendly and caring as she gave sponge baths, changed linens, emptied bedpans and brought fresh water.

Yankton was just another state institution, so like the others.

Chapter 7

There is another gap in documenting the family, but in June of 1923, nearly 14-year-old Marion was confirmed at St. Paul's Lutheran Church in Preston, Minnesota

I remember my three years of confirmation study. Mother and I often sat on the metal chairs upholstered in coral plastic around the chartreuse Formica kitchen table in our knotty-pine breakfast nook while she looked over my lessons and discussed them with me. She also listened and prompted me as I struggled to memorize Luther's Small Catechism. On the day of my confirmation, family members came to church, among them Grandma and Fred, and mother's "sisters" – Agatha, Charlotte, and Elvina and her husband, "Uncle" Gordon.

. . .

Several school report cards from Marion's years in Preston remain, all signed by Mrs. M.J. Dent. Also retained through the years was a card certifying that Marion was a member of the Girl Scouts, attaining the position of patrol leader. I, too, was a Girl Scout, and it was Mother who guided me through the requirements for the various badges.

A bill from August 1923 from the offices of Drs. Christensen & Gundersen exists noting that Carrie was charged $35 for an operation.

Another bill sent to Carrie, dated November 1925, from Dr. C.M. Quanrud, dentist, shows that professional services "For Marion, paid in full to date, $24." Did Carrie pay that bill or did Margaret give her the money?

…

Milton evidently gave up the cigar business, and documents show that in 1926 he was living in Peterson, Minnesota, giving violin lessons in Houston, Whalan, Rushford and Peterson. His pocket-sized account book shows that he received 75 cents per lesson, and the pages are filled with many names, noting addresses in various towns.

Another bill to Carrie (also from the offices of Drs. Christensen & Gundersen) survives; she was charged $250 for an operation.

Carrie evidently went to recuperate from her surgery in La Crosse, Wisconsin (most likely at her son's house).   She saved a post card from her friend, Katie, who wrote that it was "lonesome without you at the corner" (*probably the location of her restaurant*).

Marion would have been in high school during this time and was a member of the women's basketball team. It appears that Agatha was with her while Carrie was gone, as another postcard addressed to the two of them from D. Ahlstrom reads:

"This is just to let you know your mother is feeling fine and she doesn't want you to worry about her. She got your letters today & says to tell Mildred her letter was very nice. I'm keeping my promise to you so will be here until Saturday noon that will make six days.

The flowers came today and are so pretty - pink & white carnations.

There's nothing in particular she wants. She misses you. Is sitting in the corner some times when she wakes up."

…

Mother graduated in June 1927, from Preston High School, ranked third in a class of thirty.

That fall she entered Winona State Teachers College where she earned a two-year teaching degree. While there she made good friends and participated in many college activities, evidence of which (playbills, dance cards, photos, and programs from musical productions) she kept stored in a large candy box until her death. She appeared in productions of "Oh, Kay," and "Pirates of Penzance," as well as, other musical programs. Her prom dance card from 1928 is filled with twelve names and four extra names of those hoping to have a chance to dance with her.

We had a trunk at home that contained albums of pictures from Mother's years at college. They were great pictures with Mother wearing "20s-style" clothing and sporting vamp-styled hairdos. It looked to me that she had had the ultimate college experience with lots of activities and lots of friends - very much like a Rudy Vallee movie where everyone is dressed in letter sweaters, all eager for the "big game". Mother often talked about her two years at college and the friends she had made there.

Marion, upper left hand corner

I've often wondered who paid for Mother's education and the beautiful clothes she wore in pictures I've seen. Did the money that Oscar had put in an account for her add up to enough to pay her expenses Remember that in December of 1909 he agreed to deposit $375 in a bank account for

Marion and Margaret in equal shares, Marion's share to be held until she was of age. At one point he was paying Milton $5 every other week. At ten dollars a month, that debt would have been paid off in just over three years. Did Margaret use any of the money or did she save it for Marion? Certainly, Carrie, who was running a restaurant, had little money. I never heard Mother ever talk about having a job while she was at college, so I'd surmise her expenses were covered.

...

Following graduation from Winona State Teachers College, Mother accepted a teaching job in Rose Creek, Minnesota, near Austin. Her nine-month contract shows that she received $105 a month. The 1930 census records that Marion, 20, was a boarder at the home of Sylvester and Dolly Thompson, along with their sons, Lloyd, 7, and Wallace, 4, and two other teachers, Ellen Flanigan, 25, and Annette Darg, 23.

Marion replied in the census that her father was born in Wisconsin, her mother in Minnesota. Did she still believe that Milton and Carrie were her parents, or was she playing the game?

…

While Mother was beginning her teaching career, Milton's health was declining. Margaret was then at another state institution, Ah-Gwah-Ching (which means *fresh air*), near Walker, Minnesota, and the Leech Lake Indian Reservation.

After visiting family members at a lake home near Park Rapids, Minnesota, one summer, I asked Don to take me to Walker to see Ah-Gwah-Ching. We drove to the site, but nothing was there, so we returned to Walker where we had earlier spied an historical museum. While paying for tickets, I noticed a sign advertising CDs for sale, "A Historical Documentary of Ah-Gwah-Ching Sanatorium 1907-1961."

From that CD and information I gleaned at the Minnesota History Center, I learned that the treatment center, opened in 1907, was home to hundreds of tuberculosis patients who lived and worked on the property. Known then as the

Minnesota Sanitorium for Consumptives, the facility was meant to house 65 patients, but by 1927, had more than 300 patients. It boasted its own post office, railroad depot, farm, and dairy herd, and cottages for its employees. Most likely, Margaret used the train as her mode of transportation, as it appears, she never owned an automobile.

Treatment there consisted of complete bed rest: Patients were only allowed out of bed for the 10 minutes it took to change the bedding. They even ate meals from a tray that attached to the side of the bed. Fresh air was thought to be essential for treatment, so patients' beds were lined up in dormitory wings where windows were opened. In winter months they slept under layers of heavy blankets.

In the CD, some former patients told of being kept in bed for several years and of treatments that required having a very rigid tube forced down their throats.

Margaret worked at Ah-Gwah-Ching from 1930-35.

The nursing report in the facility's 1933 annual report noted that nurses worked eight-hours a day with one day off per week. The day shift worked from 7 a.m.-7 p.m. with three hours off during that period. The report from July 1, 1932- - June 30, 1933 lists 25 graduate registered nurses, four graduate nurses (Margaret was most likely a graduate nurse), eight practical nurses, and five orderlies on staff . "All nurses, orderlies, maids, dishwashers and janitors are taught and supervised in regard to contagious technique."

Medical reports speak of "collapse therapy" and patients having "pneumothorax *(a collection of air or gas in the plural cavity of the chest, between the lung and the chest wall*) established," and of patients on a fourth floor who needed "heliotherapy treatment" *(treatment of a disease by exposing the body to sunlight or specific wave lengths).*

"Thorocoplasty" *(the removal of rib sections)* and "luetic *(or syphilitic)* therapy" also are mentioned.

A report from the dietary department notes "that a girl in each kitchen is responsible for her dishes… and is charged for her breakage and losses." Inventory was taken every two weeks.

There are references to studies of tuberculosis in the Indian population, and to the construction of a separate Indian Building.

...

In 1930, while Margaret was at Ah Gwah Ching, Mother was in her first year of teaching, and my dad, who had been allowed to skip a grade of elementary school, graduated from Stewartville High School at age sixteen. His dream had always been to be a pilot, so he headed to Universal Aviation School in Minneapolis where he earned a commercial pilot's license. He spent a few years flying cargo, did some mining for gold in Montana, and then found a job at the Stewartville elevator.

...

At the close of the 1933 school year, Mother applied for a teaching position in Stewartville. The secretary of the school board wrote the following letter May 9, 1933:

My dear Miss Dent:

In reply to your note, I want to say that, so far as two of us are concerned, we feel that only one other teacher has as splendid qualifications as you. She may have signed up for something else by this time, because she was anxious to know a month ago.

Mr. Jones called me over the telephone and told me some very nice things about your ability and your splendid work in High School, especially in the Glee Club contests. His recommendation is worth a great deal. The girls who are the leaders in school naturally become the best faculty members. Average students and girls, who can't be bothered to do extra work in school, usually go on teaching in the same way.

I hope we may make a decision Friday evening. We certainly need someone of your type in our school.

Sincerely,

Elmedia Bently
(Mrs. Claude) (I remember Mrs. Bently as the organist at Zion Lutheran Church).

Just three days later, Mother received a contract to sign and return.

Mrs. Bentley wrote back May 29 -

My dear Miss Dent:

When you get ready to look for a room, let me know or come and see me.

I want you to have a pleasant home.

You know it makes such a difference what sort of a home you stay in. You will probably have letters from some of the women who are anxious to rent rooms, and of course you don't know which to choose.

Mrs. Naegle (sister of my dad's mother) of Preston is a very good friend of mine.

She called me over the telephone to tell me some nice things about you.

If you happen through here this summer, we would enjoy having you stop.

You spoke about summer school work. I don't know that I can suggest anything except that the second grade work will be just as important as the music, and the parents do watch the children's reading progression, and are always comparing progress from one year to another.

We think we have selected a good Coach,
Walford Peterson of Mankato. We still have to
choose a Dom. Science instructor as Miss Legvold
just resigned.
  I know we are going to enjoy your next year.
We haven't had a teacher with a good soprano
voice or any singing ability for a long time.
  Sincerely yours,

Elmedia Bentley
(Mrs. Claude)

A contract from the Stewartville School District
for the 1934-35 school year shows that Miss Dent
agreed "to teach Second and Third Grades, music
in the lower grades, and to perform such other
duties as the superintendent may reasonably
require of me in the administration of the school."
Her annual pay was $810.

Mother took a room with Herbert and
Magdalene Lenton (Herb was Dad's half-brother),
and that led to her meeting Dad.

In the fall of 1934 Mother began teaching in the
same school building my dad had once attended.

Newspaper clippings and old programs tell that Mother was often called upon to be a soloist at community and school events. Mixed in with her memorabilia are a few cards given to her by students. It is evident that "Miss Dent" was a beloved teacher. I have heard numerous stories about the beautiful wardrobe the dark-haired, dark-eyed, slim teacher wore, especially about the infamous "red dress," that obviously made a long-lasting impression.

Miss Dent

While Mother was starting her teaching career at Stewartville, the Dent siblings were evidently quarreling about the care of their father, Milton, whose health had declined.

...

Milton was in a Catholic care center in Minneapolis when Margaret, still in Walker, Minnesota, wrote this angry letter to Charlotte:

Charlotte:
Just a note,
Your letter (the first on in 23 months) recd.
In reply will say -
I shall have no further arguments with the family - concerning Dad.
Alvina had threatend to arrest me, have me judged insane and tried for slow murder, etc. (and judging from the content of your letter & Agatha's you all agreeing to accept her views.
I'm giving you all the chance to bring this in to Public Courts, the sooner you do, the better for me. That will be the First Chance in my life - to Prove to the Public in general - that I'm not the

"Fool" nor Brute toward my parents as you girls are all trying to paint me.

__All__ the Family letter, telegrams pretend checks will talk for me. I wont __have__ to argue.

And, as for me forcing Dad, hah. __Two__ of his own letters will __prove__ the contrary. They will also prove his is __not__ staying there against his will.

I just wonder what the Court will decide - when - they find Everyone of my letters from home were full of "family disputes not with me but among themselves," "also demands for money" - telegrams demanding the same, because they haven't the necessary means,

And then, just because I came to my Father's assistances way back in 1929 when the rest of the family ignored him when he was to be put at the Fillmore Co. poor Farm, unless someone would make good for him, and now that I'm financially down & out myself & still made the efforts to keep a Respectable Roof over his head & three square meals a day, I'm to be Considered - a Brute - toward my Aged Parents.

Alvina & Agatha were right there just a few short miles from him when this was taking place. Why didn't they come to his Assistance __no__ even his letters were ignored - just as mine are only when theres a miserable lingo or demand for Aid at the other end of the Road.

Why didnt they investigate his Conditions then? No, because they didn't give a snap.

But now, that Ive done the very best I could - they're trying to Display all my Past Efforts & Future Plans.

I suppose it is a Disgrace I have him where he has (as I've said often B.4) a Respectable Roof over his head, three square meals a day in these hard times, just because I can Keep him there for considerable less.

Sure Thoens (evidently a private home that provided care) *will find and Alibi there not getting the $80 that was coming in every month since the last part of 1929.*

Remember every cent paid Thoens was paid in check, and I have them all *so dont get excited and believe & grab every thing as* Positive Proofs *that happens to Come your way - from others, its only going to cause you, unneseccary worries.*

And as for "Slamming" & Critesizing the Catholic Home for the Aged, each & every one of you better guard your tongue.

Remember, that home is run & Supported by the Catholic Church, in other words, the Better Catholics including those in good financial standings are backing it . You may have some of those Catholics within hearing distances & they may make you - Recant your remarks & Statements. As those who support the Home, Evedently Respect their Religion and, consider where they are placing their money to spare.

 So you must all bare in mind when, you decide to try me that -

You better weigh your words, Have proof (evedence) that you are <u>all financially</u> <u>able</u> to support. That they (Mother & Dad) will never be in want while in your care.

Also, <u>Prove</u> , my that I am the Brute, in trying to neglect my Parents, & throw the Responsibility at your doors. Also be able to prove that where I sent him is "Disgrace" a "Catholic grey Walled Prison" also <u>prove</u> I sent him there to be <u>Cruel</u> to my Aged Father.

Remember, when you start this deal, it wont end in a few hot word & a door slam which seems to be as far back as I can remember - the Dent Family daily routine.

And it wont be - decided by one or two of the family favorites - But the Public & jury.

So get busy - if you have the means, all of you. I'm ready, (but, I'll let someone with ready cash start,) for I dont aim to lick the dust of family shoes - any longer. I'm not obliged to.

And, I dont intend to sit back & swallow - the Family Slam & insults.

I've shot square & I'll have justice and, the sooner you three see to it the happier I will be.

This is Final -

Dad stays at that Home until I'm financially able to place him elsewhere - if he doesn't want to - remain there after I'm on my feet he certainly dosent have to - on the other hand If he's happy & Contented Right there is where he'll stay & I'll continue paying for his keep there.

So start the Ball rolling the sooner - the quicker its settled.

And, you may as well know it now, as some time later. That's my Home also - from now on.

I'm going to at least have the satisfaction - that - when I'm ill down & out, I wont have to indure the family cold eyed stare and heated arguments - because I'm sponging on them.

And as For Matt passing his opinions - let me say this, its a Free County he can speak when & how he chooses, Well, so can I.   He's got his Hands full if he sees to <u>you</u> & <u>his</u> Children. With out bothering to throw a stumbling block in my Best Efforts.

You dident bother yourself about <u>Dad</u> <u>all</u> those past years, - Continue doing so, if you have - room & food to spare -

I have it with - Mother

Margaret

(Written upside down in the margin, Margaret continued):

Don't be silly & talk about Mother & Dad sharing the same Home. Remember Dad is divorced man. A living Wife & Child elsewhere & our Poor Old Mother - merely playing second fiddle - in his life & suffering the Consequences. If you really care for either one of them - dont- bring more suffering to them in their last years

...

What brought on Margaret's anger and her need to defend herself? Somewhere along the way, she became a Catholic. Did she change her faith to appease Milton (a lapsed Catholic) or was she swayed while working with the nuns at St. Mary's in Rochester? After so many letters in which she berated her father, suddenly she is defending him and caring for him. Is it done in spite to anger her sisters?

Either she was paying a small stipend to keep her father in the Catholic home, or he was a charity case. At that time, however, a divorced man who had married another woman could not have been considered a Catholic in good standing.

...

Mother was always close to her "immediate" family. "Aunt" Elvina and "Uncle" Gordon moved several times, but were always within thirty miles of our house. "Aunt" Charlotte and "Uncle" Matt lived in Austin, thirty-five miles away, and "Aunt" Agatha, somewhat of a recluse, lived ten miles away in Rochester. "Uncle" Clarence and "Aunt" Blanche were in LaCrosse, Wis., fifty miles away.

Mother often called Elvina, Charlotte and Agatha,
and stopped in to visit Elvina and Charlotte. No
one went to Agatha's apartment, but many times
we ran into her on the street in Rochester or in the
aisle of Weber & Judd Drug Store. She was a tiny,
fragile-looking woman, always bundled against the
elements with a buttoned-up coat or sweater and a
scarf on her head. Clarence lived farther away,
was sixteen years older than Mother and was
involved with his family of six – we saw him
infrequently. Elvina and Charlotte quarreled, and,
in later life, Agatha became very withdrawn. The
story was that Elvina had stolen her fiancé. I don't
know if that fiancé was Gordon who became
Elvina's husband.

Mother was the glue that held them all together.
We had many family gatherings at our house and
all three sisters were there. All of them loved
Wendy and me. They remembered our birthdays,
Christmas, our confirmations, graduations, and
weddings.

...

Every year, near Memorial Day, Mother, often with me along, would make a trip to Lanesboro to place flowers at the graves of Margaret and Carrie Dent. On our way up the hill to the cemetery, Mother would point out the house, set back from the street, where she had lived. Sometimes we would stop to see Lottie and Effie, a distant aunt and cousin from Carrie's side of the family.

Chapter 8

The little knife that sat on the three-tiered table next to Margaret's bed "had belonged to someone who was in a war."

That saying came back to me after discovering that my grandfather, Oscar Quarstad, had died in service to his country during WWI. My curiosity was greatly aroused. Who was this Oscar Quarstad - a man who had been in a war?

From a Fillmore County census report I learned that he was the oldest child of Odin and Wilhelmenia Quarstad, (immigrants From Norway) and that he had seven younger siblings: Emma, Agnes, Edwin, Leonard, another brother also named Leonard (I later learned that the first Leonard had drowned), Arnold and Helen. Records also noted that his father was a railroad worker.

A later census report included Oscar's widow, Cora, and the name of her son - Orval. Here was another name I had never heard, and he was my mother's half-brother!

I shared this information with Wendy and we again mulled over the whole discovery of this family secret. Where could we go from here? Were there any members of the Quarstad family living? How would we find them?

I retold this complicated family story many times over the next few years, but did nothing to dig deeper. Then one night Don was on the computer and was searching for someone's address, showing me how easy it was to track down people.

"Why don't you try to find your mother's half-brother," he said. So he typed in the name "Orval Quarstad," and immediately an address in St. Paul, Minnesota, came up.

"I don't think there could be too many people with that spelling of Orval and the last name Quarstad ," he said. "I think you found him." I was dumbfounded. My first response was to call Wendy and tell her.

"Are you going to contact him?" she asked.

"I don't know, I need to think about this," I replied.

The thought that a long-lost uncle could be living as close as St. Paul haunted me, and I had reservations about contacting him. Did he want me to find him? Was this a house address or could it be a care center?

I decided that I needed to drive to St. Paul and check out the address. It turned out to be in an area of older homes in the Highland Park district - the house was a well-maintained rambler.

I came home and spent several days composing and editing a letter.

...

I scanned the letter again and again. Did it say enough? Did it reveal too much? Would it offend anyone?

Once more I read it:

Dear Mr. Quarstad,

Researching my family history has led to you.
I have been looking for an Orval Quarstad (son of Oscar Alvin and Cora Olson Quarstad), and a search of the internet gave me your name and address.

If you are indeed this Orval Quarstad, I would very much like to talk to you. Only a few years ago, I learned, quite by accident, that my mother (who was born in 1909) was born out of wedlock, and that Oscar Alvin Quarstad of Lanesboro, Minnesota, was her father. I don't mean to cause any problems or dredge up any unpleasant memories: I am simply interested in knowing more about my heritage.

If you are the Orval Quarstad I am searching for, that would make you a half-brother to my mother and an uncle to me. I hope I have not shocked you with something you did not know.

My mother died nearly 28 years ago and there are only a few relatives left on her mother's side of the family, so I am anxious to piece as much of this story together as possible.

I would appreciate hearing from you. I live very near in Hudson, Wisconsin. You may reach me at this number.

> *Yours truly,*
> *Peggy Hale*

Deciding the letter said everything I wanted it to say, I slipped it into an envelope, addressed it, and placed a stamp in the corner.

The next afternoon, a Tuesday, I pulled up to a drive-up mailbox and reached out to drop the letter in. There was a moment of hesitation, but I let go of the letter, and as I drove away I realized that the matter was now out of my hands.

I thought about the letter several times during the next two days. Had it arrived? Would I get an answer?

. . .

Early Thursday evening the phone rang, and when I answered, a woman's voice asked for Peggy Hale.

"Speaking," I said.

"This is Emma Quarstad," she said. "My husband got your letter."

A few seconds of silence passed, neither one of us knowing what to say.

"Needless to say, we were shocked by your letter," she offered.

"Is your husband *the* Orval Quarstad I'm looking for?" I asked.

She stammered a few seconds and then asked if I had any proof of my mother's parentage.

"Yes," I replied . "I have a copy of her birth record and some letters from Oscar Quarstad to back it up. Is your husband the son of Oscar and Cora?"

"Yes, he is," she said.

The words pierced through me. I had found my mother's half-brother, a person I hadn't even known existed until a week ago!

"My husband's been sick," continued Emma, "and it's difficult for him to talk on the phone. That's why I'm making the call."

"Did he know that his father had another child?" I asked.

"No, he didn't know anything about it," she said. "We were flabbergasted."

At this point the conversation became easy, with Emma asking me about my family. Several times she was interrupted by Orval in the background who wanted her to ask particular questions.

"How did you discover this information?" she asked.

I told her about Wendy and me taking a trip to Lanesboro and happening to see the county museum along the way. I told her it was fate that a woman who worked in the genealogy room volunteered to show us how to work the system by looking up our mother's birth record.

"That wasn't fate," said Emma. "That was God, and this was meant to be.

"We'd like to meet you, and my daughter says she wants to come along, too. Could you do it on a week night?" she asked. "We don't drive anymore, so she will have to bring us, and her weekends are full."

"I'd love to meet you," I said. "Check with your daughter and let me know when it's convenient to get together."

. . .

I hung up the phone, and the reality of what had just transpired hit me. By the time I walked into the next room to tell Don about the call, I was shaking.

As soon as I had told him the complete story, I went to the phone and dialed my sister's number. She knew that I had sent a letter to Orval Quarstad.

"I just got off the phone with our Aunt Emma," I told her.

It took her a few seconds to process that information before she asked "you found *the* Orval Quarstad?"

Again I repeated the incredible story, filling her in with as much information as I had been able to absorb. I told her that they wanted to meet, and that they were interested in her, too.

We ended the call by again talking about how much that stop at the county museum had changed our lives.

Three days later, on Sunday, I returned home from an afternoon movie to find a message from Emma on my answering machine.

I called her back and she asked if it would be possible to meet the next evening. I explained that my husband, Don, had a ticket to the Timberwolves basketball game, but that I could come, and it was decided that we would meet at 7 p.m. at Bakers Square in the Highland Park area of St. Paul.

A nervous tension followed me throughout the next day as I gathered together photos and documents to share with my new family. My daughter, Martha, agreed to go with me, and so we made our way to St. Paul on a crisp winter night.

Emma had told me to ask for the "Quarstad" table at the restaurant, but when we entered, I noticed a 70ish woman with a cane (Emma had told me that she used a cane) standing with a blond woman about my age.

"Are you Emma?" I asked hesitantly.

"Peggy?" she asked back.

"Yes," I said, and she reached out and embraced me.

The blond woman also hugged me, and I noticed that her eyes had misted.

"This is my daughter, Sonia," said Emma, "your cousin."

After I introduced them to Martha, the two of them explained that Orval was waiting in the booth and that they had wanted to warn me that he was in the early stages of Alzheimer's and was rather confused about all this new relationship.

We walked to the far end of the restaurant and I was introduced to Orval, my uncle. Eighty-one-years-old, he was a slight man, with thinning hair, but his eyes were just like my mother's.

We all slid into the booth, with me seated between Emma and Orval, and from that point on, the talk became non-stop. For two and a half hours we poured over my photos and documents and through the photo album that Emma had brought along. Orval asked several times what our relationship was, but his memory of the past, of his life, his parents and his grandparents never faltered.

Orval Quarstad

Sonia and I discovered one thing after another that we had in common, and when she wrote down her address for me, I noticed that she was left-handed.

"Is anyone in your family left-handed?" she asked

"Yes, my son is," I said.

"Do you have any other left handed relatives in your history?" she inquired.

"None that I know of," I told her.

"Oscar was left-handed," she said.

We parted with hugs and promised to get together again, next time with my other three newly-found cousins, too.

The waitress who was serving us told us she "just had to ask what was going on."

"I took it that when you came into the restaurant, you didn't know each other," she said, "and now you're all laughing and having such a good time."

She loved hearing our story.

...

On the ride home Martha and I rehashed the previous hours, marveling at how comfortable it had all been. It was difficult to sleep that night as I thought about all the history I had learned, all the faces in the photos I had seen.

I am troubled by the fact that a family secret prevented my mother from ever knowing her father's family, but I feel so privileged to have the story come full circle with me.

...

Emma welcomed me as though I had always been her niece and soon invited me to lunch at her house. Orval sat at the table while Emma and I babbled on about our families and once and a while he interjected something about the past, but it was evident that Alzheimer's was taking over his short-term memory. Emma showed me through the house, pointed out family photos, and shared some old family albums with me. On the living room wall were two large, oval frames with sepia photos of Orval's great-grandparents (his mother's parents William and Ellen Wilhelmson - now my great-great grandparents).

I was told by Emma that Oscar's parents, Odin Andreassen Kvalstad *(changed to Quarstad)* and Wilhelmine Christofa Wilhelmson, both from Bodo, Norway, married in June 1887 and left on their wedding day for America. Wilhelmine, a twin, had been given at birth to her mother's childless sister and raised as her daughter.

They settled in Lanesboro where Odin secured work with the railroad.

…

That next summer, while Wendy and her husband, Dan, were visiting we invited our "newly-found" relatives to my house – Uncle Orval, Aunt Emma, and cousins Sonia (her husband, Jim, and daughter, Kim), Orval Jr. who prefers to be called "Charlie" (his wife, Sandy), Sharon, and Brian.

Wendy and I had grown up without any cousins our age (the cousins on Dad's side of the family all lived in California) and here were four cousins who had lived within sixty miles of us while we were growing up!

What a cruel trick "propriety" had played on us!

Meeting the Quarstad family caused me to again grieve for my mother's loss – denied contact with her father and never knowing her half-brother. My dad's half- brother, Herb, was a wonderful uncle, and Wendy and I had a close relationship with his wife and family. Why couldn't we have known another uncle, aunt and cousins in the same way?

Chapter 9

With Don's full support in my quest to piece together the family story, I went to Lanesboro years after discovering that Margaret was my grandmother.

It was late October and the spectacular autumn colors were waning, but the russet oaks were in their glory, and here and there a small maple stood out in scarlet profusion.

As I slowed down to enter Chatfield, I noticed the line of farm machinery at the implement dealer on my right. In an area once defined by small family farms, few implement dealerships any longer exist. As I passed through town I thought of Don's uncle and aunt who live near the high school and of my "Uncle" Gordon and "Aunt" Elvina, now long gone, who once lived in a spacious white house with a wrap-around porch only a few blocks from Main Street. Don's and my families' lives seem to have intersected many places in Southeast Minnesota.

Election signs plastered yards and the countryside as I headed into the rolling hills of the bluff country. Dust rose from a cut down cornfield where a farmer was tilling the soil. A few miles further on, another farmer was picking corn, leaving sharp edges along the still standing rows.

I drove through shadows on a road below the bluffs as the storybook town of Lanesboro came into view. Church spires and the old school building dominated the hill to the right, and the main street stretched before me. I turned left and then made a U-turn at the end of the street in order to park in front of the Cottage House Inn. I was pleasantly surprised to find that my second-floor room was tastefully decorated with antique furniture and that I had a window looking out on the main street.

After unpacking I decided to take a walk. I crossed the street and headed up Coffee Street. I am familiar with Coffee Street because on a previous trip to Lanesboro with Aunt Emma, she had pointed out the house on that street where my great-grandparents had lived. I walked the few blocks to their house and was again amazed that their large family could actually live in the tiny, red-stained house. Hearing a familiar sound, I turned to discover that there were storage bins at the end of the street and that it was a corn dryer that was making the noise. For a moment I was reminded of Dad and of what a busy season fall was for him at the grain elevator he managed. A beautiful harvest moon hung low in the sky and I wanted to linger, but the air was chilly, and I was tired, so I headed back to my room.

In the morning I headed toward a café at the intersection of the highways, but before going there I had another stop to make. I drove along the curving road up the hill to the cemetery, through the gates, turned left at the crest of the hill, and stopped the car.

I got out next to the marble marker with its photo of the young WWI army private. His eyes haunted me as much as they did the first time I saw them.

Just a few steps away I stopped in front of the ground markers that read: Carrie A. Dent, Margaret G. Dent, and Agatha Dent.

Raindrops started to fall as I got back into the warm car. Peter Ostrousko's CD was playing my favorite selection, "Heart of the Heartland," his mandolin singing a tender melody.

After breakfast I decided to drive to the Fillmore County Museum in Fountain. Rain was again beginning to fall, and the day became very dreary by the time I reached Preston. Just a few blocks from the courthouse in this town's square, my dad's Aunt Minnie (the Mrs. Nagle who had spoken kindly of Mother when she applied for a teaching job in Stewartville) had a millinery shop in her home. She also played the piano for silent movies in the theater across the street, and later, when "talkies" came into vogue, sold tickets from the glassed-in booth at the front of the theater.

Once again on Highway 52, I drove toward Fountain, passing the office where Don and I once were cleared for a loan to buy his uncle's farm. We had a change of heart at the last minute, but I've often wondered how our lives would have been had we chosen to buy the 640-acre farm that had once belonged to his grandfather. Rain was falling hard by that time and I was glad when I could finally turn off for the museum.

A woman appeared as soon as I was though the door, and I asked to use the history resource room. She led me to a room I had visited twice before, gave me a few instructions, and for the next two hours I was lost in card files and microfiche.

Back on the road to Lanesboro I passed the field that had been filled with activity yesterday. But now a corn picker and two tractors with wagons stood silent: The corn was wet. There wouldn't be any picking that day.

On my return to Lanesboro, I warmed up in my room and then decided to browse the downtown shops. Once a railroad town, Lanesboro went through some difficult years before being reborn as a tourist town. Many of its storefronts are old, some dating back to the late 1800s, and I became conscious that three generations of my family had probably crossed over some of the thresholds.

I could easily imagine Mother, coming down the hill from the school and stopping in at Carrie's restaurant.

…

Lanesboro continued to draw me.

I had another stay there one April – a birthday present from Don. In early spring Lanesboro was a sleepy town, not yet bustling with tourists. Trees were already turning green that year, tulips were in full splendor, fields had been plowed, and the Root River was flowing freely.

I drove to the cemetery, again to see the graves of Oscar and Margaret and Margaret's mother, Carrie.

Curious about Carrie's family, I decided to investigate that branch of the family at the Fillmore County Museum. The woman in charge brought me the census records for 1880, and I discovered that Carrie, her parents, Gilbert and Kari (I had been led to believe that her mother's name was Karen) Ellingson, and her brother, Ole, had lived in Pilot Mound. The 1890 census placed Carrie (age 18) in Chatfield. I was sorry to learn that the 1900 census records were destroyed in a fire, creating a gap in her story.

While I was sitting at the table a woman came in carrying some large rolled up papers. She spread them on another table and she and the museum clerk got into a discussion about a plot of land that contained a family burial plot. The gist of the conversation was that the woman wanted to be buried there, but there was no cemetery association, so where did she need to get permission for future burials?

"Do you think I'm crazy?" she asked the clerk.

"Absolutely not," replied the clerk. "People think I'm crazy to do this job. They just don't get it. They just don't get it!"

I smiled at their comments, thinking about my family members who didn't understand my obsession with this story.

After checking the card file, I discovered that Kari Bergsrud Ellingson's 1905 obituary was in a Lanesboro newspaper. I read it and learned that she was survived by son, Ole, daughter, Carrie, and two other daughters only referred to by their married titles. The obituary said she was buried in the Root Prairie Lutheran Church Cemetery. I asked directions, barley drove out of town, and spied a sign pointing me to the church. Just a few miles from Fountain, the white wooden church has an imposing site atop one of the countryside's rolling hills. I parked the car and begin walking between the rows of tombstones, most of them baring Norwegian names. I was nearly to the top of the hill when a weathered, mold-covered vertical stone with the word "Bergsrud" at its base caught my eye. At the top was the name "Kari" followed by the dates of her birth and death. Why was the name "Bergsrud" on the stone;

"Ellingson," her married name was nowhere noted. Was it a Norwegian custom to list a woman's maiden name or was she divorced? (I did look for her husband's name in the museum card file, but there was no information on him). I stared at the marker thinking that this woman was my great-great grandmother who came to America with her husband in 1852. What would she have thought about her daughter Carrie's troubled marriage?

I walked the town of Lanesboro that day, almost to the top of the hill where the Lutheran church and the old school stand; up Coffee Street, noting the building where Milton likely made cigars and the tiny home where Oscar grew up (mere blocks apart); across the walking bridge that spans the Root River (the river that claimed the life of one of Oscar's brothers: Nine-year-old Leonard Quarstad drowned while playing on the floating ice chunks with a friend), and past the ball park where Oscar (or "Mike," as he preferred to be called) probably honed his skills.

Their lives haunted me.

Chapter 10

Memory problems overtook my newfound Uncle Orv shortly after I met him, and he took up residence in the Minnesota Veterans Home. Orv had served in World War II (N. Africa, England, Ireland, Scotland, and Italy) and was awarded the Purple Heart; he retired from the St. Paul Post Office and was a long-time friend of Bill W.

Orval Quarstad, WWII

Don and I went with Emma to visit him on one
occasion, and another time, I picked up Emma and
we went to visit him, shortly after his diagnosis of
cancer. He was sitting with a group of other men,
but we were encouraged to go into the room. We
caught Orv's eye as we took seats in the back of
the room, and I was situated where he and I could
see each other. The group leader was discussing
something from past years – as I recall, it was train
cars - and the residents were encouraged to join in
the discussion. Orv cast a glace my way several
times. Did he know who I was?

Afterward, he was scheduled for his first
radiation treatment for cancer and was led to a bus
that would take him across the campus. Emma and
I followed in the car. It was a very short wait: He
was in and out in minutes. He was then
transported back to his residence, and again Emma
and I followed in the car. After a short visit in his
room, I said my good-bye with a kiss on his cheek.

A few days later, Don and I left for our month-
long stay in Florida via Ohio where we planned to
visit his aunt and uncle. We had barely arrived in
Dayton when I received a call from Emma telling
me that Orv had passed away. I was saddened that

I wouldn't be at his funeral, but thankful that I had seen him recently.

The obituary Emma posted read: "preceded in death by parents, Oscar and Cora; brothers, Kenneth and Douglas Peterson *(his mother remarried)*; sisters, Donice Knothe and Marion Lenton."

Mother's identity was public.

In the summer of 1934, Margaret wrote an angry letter to Charlotte:

Dear Sister: - (So the Buble & the Preachers say)

But oweing to the fact that I'm not writting a very pleasant letter - I'll say no more in regards to the Phrase.

I may as well get down to Brass tacks with you as well as I have the Rest.

(Its concerning Mother).

You recall about 3 years ago Four of you - The Twins - yourself and Marian wrote me some mighty insulting letters.

Terming me - mentally unbalanced & Cruel & unjust in regards to my Aged Parent.

You made a Public Scene by trying to make me out a fool - accusing me of Disgracing you all -

*beyond indurance. In other words my act was
either of one insane - & needed to be pittied or -
unpardonably Cruel.*

*Ther was also a Threat made by all of you.
Id never get the Chance to treat Mother so.
You'd prove to the world - what I was and you'd
also Prove to the World what Love and Respect
you had for your Aged Parents. ha ha*

*You'd sacrifice everything - to your last Crust
of Bread & if your home were only a hut - there'd
be Room for Mother. Ha ha*

*"you'd never think of" nor would "any one
ever get a chance to say about you Four what was
said about me" - no?*

*Dont forget - little Lady - the Public you
worried about before - isent blind to your Acts any
more then they were to mine.*

*And, I had & still have my Fathers Request - for
Aid - owing to his Age & health -*

*I also have his letters and Mrs Thoes also that
he wrote to you all - but that the letters were
ignored.*

*Yet what did I get from the Family - as an act of
thanks for - granting him his Requests & sparing
you?*

Laughable isent it.

And now - what are you merciful daughters - Doing for your Mother in her last days. Surely you wouldent send her to a Home among strangers. That would be Cruel & inhuman for fact an insane act -

No One with Sense would do that and if you did where would the Love & Respect for your Father & Mother come in - what would People think the one that wer so ashamed of my conduct.

(Father - "Our Father" as you stated in your letter was threatened so not given a chance to talk for himself - Stuck behind the Bars of that Catholic Prison)

But Mother - thats different. She's <u>never</u> Suffered - Wept nor worried over you Four and your welfare.

She walked up & down Easy Street & you poor things - suffered - you were cold, hungry - unkept & left uneducated.

What a life you'd all had if your Mother had stayed by and sacrificed a little of her selfishness.

Surely - this must be your feeling toward her - now that shes down & out or you wouldent have the Guts to say & Act as you do. And surely

because of her Old Aged - Mental & Physical
Condition you'd die B. 4. You'd place her in an
Asylum.

Not that you'd care - (your actions in the Past
have proved it). But - think of the Stigma on
yourself - your Future and your children and their
Future.

Quite a Problem isent it.

And to - Quoting your own letter here -
"(And supposing the Building would burn" like
that one somewhere in the West - just think what
you'd have on your Soul (that is if you have any to
answer for)

By restoring your Husbands health - and give
him a chance to live & Earn as he did in the Past
you can plan Sceme & hurt others to meet your
own gains - thats your Privlige. But Remember -
Christ said "with what Measures ye meet - shall ye
be met) if not here, hereafter so you better think
twice – Margaret

...

Carrie's health, too, declined, and a June 1934
letter from Elvina to Charlotte notes that she was
being cared for at Charlotte's home.

Elvina wrote: *"I got a nasty letter from Margaret Saturday saying somebody <u>white</u>* (presumably a nurse*) had told her we were not treating Mother squarely and giving all kinds of threats. I guess she didn't know Mother was up there with you... I know she is just trying to scrape up some trouble so I am not answering her letters. Her conscience is guilty that's all and she would love to get some more sorrow over us.*

If she would do the square thing herself I would see that she does her share too for Mother probably that would stop her complaining, but I know she would do the same as she did to Pa - put it over for someone else to do.

This is what is making her mad because she has nothing to say about it, and she won't if I have anything to say."

...

Reading through the packet of letters that fell into my hands, I became aware of a side of Elvina that I had never known. Her letters to Margaret are vindictive - reminding Margaret of the shame she brought upon the family. Other letters to her sister, Charlotte, accuse Charlotte of not doing her share for their mother.

Elvina had a good relationship with my mother, Margaret's child. I don't know that she ever said anything to my mother about being born out of wedlock.

One of the letters makes me sympathize with Elvina. Pleading with Charlotte to help care for their mother, she says that Gordon has been out of work and they barely have food to feed their five children. I know times were difficult then, and I heard her daughter, Geraldine, once comment about how hard "daddy" had worked to support their family.

Elvina's harsh words in her letters are part of Margaret's story, but I don't want to paint a bad impression of Elvina because of a few letters. She was a loving "aunt" to me.

...

In July 1934, Marion wrote to Charlotte from Chicago where she was attending the Century of Progress World's Fair. She told about the fair, about going to a show, and about having a tour of

Chicago. Then she wrote: *"Your letter was surprising, Charlotte. I know you think I'm responsible for whatever Margaret wrote. I can't say anything that will convince you otherwise. But you'd have to think me pretty low if you think I'd write & rave and say horrid things about Matt & you - after I've made my home there for several years. I don't really think you could believe that of me. It isn't so and regardless of what you think about it - I know, so I can't feel that I'm that bad. I know I haven't done it. Whatever she said, I don't know - it's rather difficult - after all - I can't help what she does. I can't help that I try to like everyone and I do try to please all. I've always thot quite a great deal of you & Matt & your children - You never seem to believe that either - and I think a lot of her too - after all I should, shouldn't I? - but no matter about that - I have never been disloyal about anything - and I've always, if anything, told my appreciation for things. So whether you believe that or not - it's true -*

She concludes by giving an address in Minneapolis where she will be staying while looking for (summer) work.

Love,
Marion

...

What accusations did Margaret make against her own daughter? And why did Charlotte question Marion's love?

This letter is the first written proof I have that Mother acknowledged Margaret as her mother. When she found out that Margaret was her mother, I don't know.

...

In July, 1934, Margaret wrote to her mother (who was residing with Charlotte in Austin):

Dear Mother : -

Just a line - to let you see - I think of you - Hope your well & happy.

And if for any reason blue - Brace up - putting your Hopes - that and future intrests - in Gods Care. He wont disappoint you.

Sent you a small box of hard candy yesterday. I remember you telling me in the Past - that was the kind you enjoyed keeping in your pocket.

Love, Margaret

Written in the margin: *Im <u>still wondering</u> - if you got the Mother Day box I sent you.*

…

An undated letter with only the 1934 postmark visible was sent to Carrie (residing with Charlotte) from Margaret who was still living in the nurses' home at the Ah-Gwah-Ching state facility. She wrote:

Dear Mother: -

Just a line to let you know - I havent forgotten you

altho I have rec'd no answer - when sending Gift Pakages & Cards.

I hold no ill will.

I realize the circumstances (Carrie was suffering from dementia) *And all I hope & Pray is that the Good Lord will see fit - and soon - to release you - of all your heartaches and mental and Physical suffering.*

He understands - even tho those who are supposed to be near & Dear to - fail to see.

I havent seen you for almost Eight years and the Lord only knows if I'll ever see you in this hard old World.

But - bare in mind Mother -

Not one day in my Life has ever gone by That I havent regretted the heartaches & worries I've caused you.

Nor has one day gone by that I havent asked God to watch over you & keep you. And that altho we may never see each other here

We'll meet where - no one can separate us. & where Christ will be our Ever lasting hope & Joy.

God Bless you,

Margaret

How sad that Margaret hadn't seen her mother for eight years. They were living in the same state. Was it distance that separated them or had their relationship become deeply fractured?

...

Meanwhile, Milton remained at the Catholic home in Minneapolis for at least four years, and died August 13, 1935. His death certificate indicates that was under a doctor's care for eight months and that he died of a cerebral hemorrhage to the right temple side. The certificate also records that he last worked as a musician ten years prior to his death.

His body was taken to Portage for burial in the Dent family plot.

...

In a letter written to Charlotte shortly after Milton's death, Margaret, who was living at 205 ½ E. Hennepin Street in Minneapolis, had her name on a nurses' registry, and was waiting for work. She wrote:

"Have only offered one case since my return & gosh the folks I stayed with dident get word to me in time - so I lost out.

Have chg. My add. Now. Its somewhat depressing her but, the Phone is right out side my Door & the office Girl has promised to notify me at once - when I get a Call...

Some how I feel that the last few months have put a Cramp on me

I'm not down in the Dumps but I simply cannot make any head way it seems. I only hope the next few weeks hold something worthwhile in store for me. something I able to do.

There's plenty to do but I cant make the Grade - just now.

So I'm going to grab the first offer when I feel half way capable - and bring wages."

She talks about seeing someone they know whose uncle died recently at the Home and closes by saying *"Saw the Nuns Sunday P.M."* (I assume she is talking about the Catholic home where Milton died and the nuns there).

The letter seems very rational and friendly. Margaret evidently is having health problems that are hindering her nursing ability. Did she have to leave her job at the state hospital near Leech Lake?

...

Milton's funeral expenses appear to have been paid by Margaret and Charlotte and Matt. In January 1936, Margaret, who was then working at a convalescent home at 1327 Emerson Avenue in Minneapolis, sent a receipt to Charlotte that said:

"This is to - Certify - that the Agreement of Paying Fifty ($50.00) Dollars toward Father's Funeral Expenses Have been - by - matt & Charl. Darr

Paid in Full.

Margaret G. Dent

Included with the receipt was a letter:

Dear Charlotte: -

Your ever welcomed letter rec'd. also check.

Yes, this your Final Payment in other words your thru...

Sent her (Clarence's wife who was caring for Carrie in their home) *$25 today - just got part of my check. Asked for it for fact - as I needed it so badly.*

Wish I could see you folks - including Marion - Dont suppose you could drive up do you. If you do tho be sure and let me know - when your coming. Will write you again in regards to this matter in a Day or two. Its concerning a letter I got from Clarence.

But I expect another & when I get it I'll write you - or if its anything hasty might - Phone you some Eve.

Do you hear from Alvina: if so, How is she?
I'm working now - in a Convalescence Home - a
Rest Hospital.
   Only 9 pat's so far.
   But it very Expensive.
   Specialized a Reg. Nurse the first week I was
here day & night.
   They're mostly all Nervous Break Downs &
Aged that are here
    is really a wonderful place. Dont know how
long I'm here but I sure like it - I was only hired
indefinately.
   Hope I'll get steady work - soon.
  Write & Soon -
  all I look forward to - in my Past-time is the mail,
  Love,
Margaret

...

That July, Margaret again wrote to Charlotte:

Dear Sis: -
   Your card is a Shock to me.
   I dont understand what its all about.

You speak of a letter when did you write it and did you add it to 1926 - 5th - Ave So?

They are slow & indifferent in forwarding mail. But - I've been over ther since & she said (the ManagerI mean) there was no other mail than a card from Lax. Which she gave me.

the card was from Blanche giving me thery're new add. I havent heard from Marian. I've written twice add. It where I thot she might be but I've had no reply.

So I'm beginning to believe I dont know where she is.

Wish I knew all this letter had to tell me - you wrote that so far I've never got.

When you feel better (as I know by your card theres been something wrong. And I sincerely hope you are on the Road to a Rapid Recovery.

Your card written with Pencil - some parts of it is so bright I couldent make it out...

Hope the move Clarence's have made has been to their better Advantages & that Mother wont be so crowded in. Do you know where 1013 Calendonia St. is? Or maybe you dont know any more about Lax than I do.

Where is Agatha. Do you know?

Well, now I'm going to come to my own troubles.

I'm feeling better - but dreadfully uncertain and still getting my "Hypo"

the Dr. claims the Hypos have brought about a great change and improvement.

The Blood Pressure has been brought down 50 points, the Systalic Rate Sixty.

He claims the greater part of the complete cure is up to me -

To obey his orders - that should I neglect in doing so - only shortens my life...

I tried going against his Order by accepting work that I felt wasent hard & the results were almost hopless.

He claims general examination - proved so near a stroke -

He cant understand himself - how I escaped. He said if ther is such a thing miracles - there was one performed in my case, so in one sense Im mighty thankful.

I'd gladly accept Death -

To a Stroke where I'd perhaps live for years in a chair or Bed.

He feels concerned if I Live as he advises I'll come out of this & be O.K.

You can feature what crossed my mind - when he said - "I must be honest with you - your in the Red, chances Poor -

there's no use in placing you on false hopes. Poor Old Dad flashed thru my mind so strong - I hardly heard what else he had to say.

As I'm writing theres one thing I feel mighty thankful for & that is - that Dreadful Rush & Hum in my Right Ear is disappearing. I notice it considerable less today than yesterday...

My - there nice to me here. I dont know what in Gods world I'd do if I wasn't so fortunate as to have found them in my Searching for Rooms.

Its a Hotel -

But - so clean - home like & friendly. And each time I've been ill - they given meals in order to spare me climbing the stairs.

I wouldent get that otherwise - as they dont serve - only Rooms.

Marion was here one night with me.

Dont know what she thot of them.

Saw the Supt. From Walker the other Day he said I should come back - when my health was Better & the Insurance Co. was Settled in Full.

Well, now to my real reason - for writing you this morning.

Circumstances are Draining me - be side my self.

Will you send me $35.00 - at once.

A Loan understand until I get some more from the Insurance Co. and Please don't doubt or fear in getting it back. And I know the Good Lord will reward you - in more ways then one.

As I need it so badly - for several different necessities - Medecines, ect. & my Room rent.

When I get my money I'll give one Dollar on every five. And I may get it in a Mo. If not, I'll consider this length of the Loan & act accordingly. (so please consider I'm so in need). I hope you understand (& youll get it back with out Question) Love Margaret

. . .

Inside a greeting card with the picture of two little angels putting a letter in the mailbox, the

printed words "Somebody loves you," Margaret
wrote to Mother in an undated note:

Dear Marion:

Got your nice long letter last eve.

*So glad to hear – but realize your busy & need
all the rest you can get – so I understand alright
the only thing I hope I can depend on – is – if all
things don't go well – phone & Special – if I can
depend on that.*

*Then I wont mind – see I'll write a long letter to
nite – Monday - you should get the letter Wed.
mail as well as telephoning here a problem.*

*Too many handle it to send me & sometimes I
feel concerned my mail has been handled and
ther's a couple here I don't trust – but not trusting
isn't fact – so – one just has to wonder.*

By until tonite.

*P.S. You supposed to be well on the road to
recovery – but seeing your not this card I guess
was appropriate.*

Marg

...

After several years of ill health and dementia while being cared for by Elvina, Charlotte, and Clarence's wife Blanche, Carrie died on her 75th birthday, November 13, 1936, in a La Crosse hospital. Her funeral was held in Bethlehem Lutheran Church, Lanesboro, and she was buried in the Lanesboro cemetery in one of the four plots that were purchased by Charlotte and Matt. Margaret and Agatha were later buried in two other plots.

Carrie's death certificate lists her occupation as "a housewife" - there is no mention of the years she spent managing the candy store in Rushford or the many years she earned her living running a restaurant in Lanesboro and then in Preston.

Chapter 11

Just a few short weeks later, in a special delivery letter sent from Fair Oaks Sanitorium in Wadena, Minnesota, where Margaret spent her remaining nursing years, she wrote to Charlotte:

Dear Folks: -

Well, here's hoping I can keep my thots collected enough on one subject or two, long enough to write what I've thot of every day since I got back....

She writes that she is sorry to hear that Charlotte is bedridden and advises her to follow doctor's orders and perhaps to consult at the clinic in Rochester.

You are my Sister - there's an interest that one cant - just explain and then to, your young - Every thing in the World to live for - a Husband & family - in other words a Real Home of which you are a very important part with years of Happiness ahead of you when you get your health back.

I certainly felt sorry for you those last few days I saw you, but feeling sorry dident relieve your distress - or make the burdens any lighter so, I dident say anything.

Well, now to the Business side -

The Funeral Expenses

Marion & I discussed the matter the evening we there with Matt - but I believe it was only one point I got definite and that was - that Marion & I send Matt our checks - just as you folks & Marion sent yours to me last year.

Because Matt signed up - just as I did.

But this is the question.

You remember I asked Mr. nelson if $10.00 a Mo. Was satisfactory and he said yes.

Just what was the intire bill - I tried to figure it out - or rather I tried to Remember what I was told it was - But I cant.

It was understood that you folks - Marion & I will foot the Bill - in other word we each pay 1/3 of the Full Bill (including everything) the way I have it figured (if I remember right to Eighty some odd Dollars a piece. Am I right?

And here's the next point seeing he agreed on $10.00 a Mo.

Can we just pay the $10 a month for the next two - Marion pd, or Do you feel that there should be $20 - $10 from each of us.

I'm confident it wouldn't make any difference to him just so he got a check each Mo. At least not for the first two or three months.

You see I've only worked since Oct. 3rd. and I had to borrow money to get to the funeral so you see I'm sort of pinched.

Those girls & the Dr's wife expects at least part of what they personally loaned me.

But there one thing you can be <u>assured</u> of that there'll always be a check, unless Im flat on my back.

The letter is continued the next day:

Dont guess Ill ever get this letter written - just as I got well under way one of my patients sprung a hemmorage and Ive been kept busy with her - with all my other General work so I just had to put this a side until I went off duty ...

B4 We left that morning for Lanesboro were discussing Mother's trunk and its contents.

I believe I told you - yet I may have forgotten to - that -

I took - my hair (you see I may get a chance to sell it) a Pin Cushion a bright blue Crochet top - I gave Mother while at Yankton, A tiny snap she had of Marion in a little blue box, 5 Hkfs - 4 new ones, 1 old one, and one of my vases I got from Sam Nelson years ago in Sunday School & Mother's Picture (mine).

I did pick out some other things but put them back - because I didn't have anything but that small brown Hand bag and I couldent get them in They were things of Marion's when she was a Baby that I felt <u>no</u> <u>one</u> but me would care the least bit for. (I still have a pair of her small leather shoes with button straps).

So as you said when we left - the trunk was alright there in the attic but in case you moved - you perhaps wouldent have space you have now.

When I have the Price of Fare to Austin I would like to come down & we'd go thru it together & then what you want - take & then I'll take the trunk back with me.

The Different things that belong to Agatha-Alvina - Marion & Clarence.

*I can easily pick out - Wrap them separate &
send them to them or keep them until they do want
them*

*I believe we'd all like some little keepsake of
Mother's & I believe I already have mine - Her
Photo - the 5 Hkfs and that Red Knit throw I gave
her while working at Yankton & which she has
used the last Couple of years Quite a lot.*

*There's only one thing I feel guilty of & thats
the Hkf's others may want them - & yet such things
really aren't keepsakes as they're often used & lost
& I need Hkfs so darn bad - its a Pity...*

*I'll sure be glad when I can get all my Pictures
there in the Box - you spoke having them all put in
Mother's trunk - well, that would be fine only
Perhaps it would be good Policy to go thru it
together - & then together may not be Room - as it
is now...*

Love

Marg

*P.S. The $35.00 I owe you, will be Paid seperatly
from the check sent for Burial Expenses. Will try
to have it all Paid in 6 months.*

The following letter to Charlotte and Matt also was sent from Wadena:

Jan. 3-37
Dear Folks;-
Just a line – hope this letter finds everything or rather everybody feeling fine.
Wrote Charlotte twice but so far no reply so really don't know how she is or where she is. If at home or still at the Hospital. Well, now that its over I hope everything going to be O.K.
That there'll be no further operations or that her Health will be built up to the point that she can actually feel strong & get some Happiness out of life.
Am sending you $20.00 Matt – apply it where ever you see fit
Either Nelsons – or – toward the $35.00 borrowed.
And when you feel like it & have the time _ Give me exact Amt – toward Mothers expenses. Its $80.00 or in that range. You see Matt my reason for asking
My Health isn't the Best -& one never knows whats ahead

And all I have is –

My Earnings and a small amt in a Belvolent Society to back me.

So you see I'd like to have all my Debts – Down in Black & White.

Just now – its My share toward Mothers Expenses.

The amt barrowed from you folks $35.00 and the $120.00 borrowed to pay Blanche off the ninty I owed her for the months I was laid up & not working –

So you can see my Reason for wanting to know Just where I stand.

If I were drawing a big check & my Health O.K.

I wouldent care – but as it is – it would only be fair to all concerned.

If Char is Home & able, have her write me. I'd enjoy hearing

Tell the Girls "Hello." That I wish you all a Happy New Year

Love, Margaret

Chapter 12

I know that Mother had many suitors during
her college and teaching years (one who even
promised a honeymoon in Brazil), and that it took
time for my Dad to win her over. Even though he
was several years younger, she eventually said
"yes" to him.

Among letters that were saved in my parents'
home was this one, dated on a Monday, in either
1937 or 1938:

Darling,

*I'm still so thrilled I'm fairly walking on air –
could you understand that? The ring is beautiful,
since I've caught my breath and really looked, I'm
better able to go into raptures, you see. You can
surprise me after all. Everyone thot it lovely and
seemed not very surprised – must be they knew I
was serious – spose? I even awakened them*
(probably Dad's half brother, Herb, and his wife,
Mag who were her landlords) *to show them – and
they responded beautifully. I'm really so happy – I
was before, but it seems so much more real now…*

*Just finished the dishes! I peeled the potatoes
for supper too. I can do both of those and sew on
buttons. Is that enough besides loving you beyond
all limits...*
Yours,
Marion

...

Mother and Dad were married June 29, 1938, 8
p.m., in St. Olaf Lutheran Church in Austin,
Minnesota – the same church where her father,
Oscar, had married Cora Olson. My "Uncle" Matt,
husband of "Aunt" Charlotte, walked her down the
aisle. Mother's maid of honor was a friend,
Margaret Moran; Dad's half-brother, Herb, was his
best man, and Dad's brother, Bob, and Dad's
sister, Anita, also were among the wedding party.

According to a newspaper article that Mother
had saved, the bridesmaids wore "matching frocks
of aqua silk organdie with short net veils of
matching shade. They carried colonial bouquets of
pink sweet peas and roses."

"White satin with lace insets made on princess
style was worn by the bride, whose fingertip-

length veil was held with a lace cap. She carried gardenias.

"Fifty guests were entertained at a reception at the Y.W.C.A. following the ceremony and a three-course luncheon was served cafeteria style." Several out-of-town guests, including Dad's mother, are listed in the newspaper write up, but there is no mention of Margaret. Is it possible that she wasn't there or was her name merely omitted? The description of the bride's dress fails to paint the image of its body-clinging, Jean Harlow style of the '30s. Fifty-one years later, my daughter, Martha, walked down the aisle in her grandmother's dress, bringing tears to Dad's eyes.

Wendell & Marion Lenton

The final letter from Margaret addressed to Charlotte, that was among the papers tied with the blood-red cord, that has linked Mother's family together also was postmarked from Wadena.

> *Jan 1 –41*
> *5:00 a.m.*

Dear Sis:-

I've just got to drop a line –

Thank you folks for those beautiful nylon Hose (something I've always wanted – since they were put on the market & felt I couldn't afford)

And all the same time To Wish You all a Happy New Year.

I read your card and will write a letter soon.

Was glad to hear you all enjoyed Xmas.

I did – very well – considering.

But when ones strength is all sapped out of them – theyre real mental interest seems to be lacking to.

Tho I must admit I seem to be gradually getting better.

At least I hope I am –

I'm still miserbly weak and am actually drenched with persperation with the slightest exertion.

Altho the pleurisy is practically gone. That throat irritation – seems to hang on. Yet I must admit its much better.

Am making plans for a General Checkup as soon as I can make necessary arrangements. But this weather seems to have an awful effect on me – so I'm waiting until it sort of gets clear and colder. Will write you – when I find out facts – Love to all

Marg

. . .

A few years later, Margaret came to live with us in Stewartville, taking up residence in the small bedroom at that top of the stairs. There is no record of exactly how long she lived with us and no one left to ask. Wendy estimates that she was with us four to five years.

She remembers going into Margaret's room to visit with her and recollects times when Margaret sat in the kitchen. She has a vivid memory of a time she and Leona and Margaret were sitting at the kitchen table and Margaret made mention that she probably had a half-sister somewhere.

She did.

Frannie Dent from her father's first marriage lived with her grandmother as a youngster in the same county as the Dent family. Did they ever cross paths? Did Milton ever see her? Did he pay any child support?

Census records revealed that after she was married, Frannie Parker lived in Chicago, Ft. Worth, and Los Angles. She died July 20, 1970 in Butte, California.

…

Wendy also remembers that prior to her birthdays or Christmas Margaret would ask her to look through the Sears and Montgomery Ward catalogs and pick out some items she might want.

Wendy, Mother & Margaret

…

My fondest memory of Margaret was being called to her room when it was time for "Big John and Little Sparky" sitting on the floor of her room inhaling the citrus scent from the orange peels on the radiator, looking at the three-tiered table next to her that held the familiar green glass water carafe with the tumbler that fit upside down on its neck, the black case with the syringes, Margaret's book and Bible, her rosary, the black wooden cross with the plastic Jesus, and the little knife that "had belonged to a man who was in a war."

Margaret died in February 1952, leaving her forty-two year-old daughter, a son-in-law, and two granddaughters, eleven and five. Mother was the informant on her death certificate and listed Margaret's usual occupation as "housework."

What made her omit a lifetime of nursing?

Chapter 13

Christmas, 1960 – Wendy, Me, Mother
Grandma Aletta holding Wendy's daughter Carrie,
"Grandpa" Fred, and Dad

...

In the late winter or early spring of 1972 my
mother was hospitalized at Methodist Hospital in
Rochester. The prior summer, she had undergone
surgery for colon cancer, had regained her strength

and had gone back to teach that fall. But she didn't return after the Christmas break. Her cancer had advanced.

My dad, my sister, Wendy, and I were taking turns sitting with her. I remember one instance while I was with her that a nurse came into my mother's room and Mother introduced me to the nearly middle-aged woman, telling me that she had recently returned to school to earn her degree.

"I always wished that I had been a nurse," my mother announced, revealing something I had never before known.

I also distinctly remember one snowy afternoon while sitting with Mother that I was lost in a historical novel, set in Ireland. Mother was dozing, sometimes muttering while I was in the midst of a rugged landscape with a castle perched on a cliff above angry seas . I was deeply drawn into the story of a handsome Irish lord who was in love with a woman of lowly stature when my mother suddenly blurted out:

"And there was my father, dead at the bottom of the steps and I vowed then that I would find his killer."

I looked up from my book, stunned. Where did that come from? Was she hallucinating?

I shared Mother's words with my sister and we attributed them to her condition and the drugs that had been administered.

But the words reverberated sharply when, years later, I saw a copy of Milton's death certificate. He died eight months after suffering a cerebral hemorrhage to the right temple area, and a check mark was made next to "If death was due to external cause (violence) - accident, suicide, or homicide."

The matter remains a mystery.

Margaret Dent of Walker, Minnesota was the informant on the certificate.

...

Margaret's trunk and few possessions moved with my parents to their new home in 1967 and remained there until my stepmother sold the house in 1990, a year after Dad's death. She and Wendy had weeded through family memorabilia (I was living in Belgium at the time), had set aside some things for me, and had taken them to Don's brother's house to store until my return.

While visiting there for Christmas, my son and I went into the spare bedroom to see what had been packed away for me. The black wooden cross with the white plastic Jesus slid out beneath some pictures when I opened a box.

Margaret's worn and tattered small bible also came into my possession. Written in pencil on the black insides of the covers are these words:

"I have done lots of wrong. I know the Lord will forgive me if I ask earnestly, and that I do.
Have patients with me O Lord."

...

Jaci, my friend since second grade, sent me a beautiful letter after I shared my mother's story with her. She lost her mother while we were in junior high school and came to think of Mother as a second mother. She wrote:

"That was certainly quite the information you shared in your last letter concerning your mom. I wonder when Marion found out that Aunt

Margaret was really her mother and I wonder if your dad knew. I wonder if she confided in any of her friends and shared her feeling with them. It would be interesting to know how all of this influenced Marion's views of life and self. Secrets always take their toll and every family has them. Consider the time frame of white gloves and hats and propriety and how difficult that all could have been. What was her life like growing up? Was it a happy one being raised by the grandparents? Can you imagine her dedication to seeing that Wendy and you had all the security and respectability that perhaps she felt had been missing for her? And think of the extreme pride she took in all of your accomplishments. It is so interesting to see all that goes into making us who we are and just what a great influence our childhood and upbringing are on the person we become and the way we raise our children.

Your dad has always been your hero, but I'm thinking that mom of yours was pretty remarkable and full of unsung courage, dedication and determination. I loved her dearly and am so thankful for the positive influence she always had on my life."

...

I, too, now think she was pretty remarkable. Not knowing her background or fully realizing the family dynamics among her "siblings" during the years that I knew them, I am in awe of the confident, intelligent, poised, caring woman I knew as "Mother."

I can't help but believe that all this family information came to me for a reason – to tie the story together, to know my grandmother, and to gain a better understanding of my mother. She never read all the papers that came tied with red cord – never truly knew her own story. I now marvel at the guilt and angst she must have kept bottled up inside her while I knew her as a loving mother, concerned teacher, dedicated Christian, and involved citizen. She and Dad were both pillars of our church and our small community.

They didn't argue often, but I remember Dad admonishing on more than one occasion that "you always have to have the last word." And she did.

Both Wendy and I recall that Mother had great concern whenever she heard about a teenage pregnancy. I now understand her true concern for that girl and her child. How difficult it must have been for her, not to relate her own story.

Mother also was a strong advocate for education, warning us "that you never know when you might have to support yourself."

A few days after Christmas of my eighteenth year, I came home from a date with Don showing off the diamond that he had given me. Mother broke into tears, not because she didn't like Don - she did love him - but that it meant I probably would not continue my college education. (I did leave college after two years, but seventeen years later went back and attained a degree in journalism. Mother wasn't there to share that accomplishment, but I knew she would have been proud of me).

I was very uncomfortable in junior high school having Mother as my geography and English teacher, but it gave me the opportunity to see her as a professional who expected the best from her students and who truly cared about those who came from disadvantaged backgrounds. Every year she showed the film "A Desk for Billy," the story of a girl whose parents were migrant workers, a girl who never had a real home, a girl who drifted from school to school who found self confidence through a teacher who really cared about her. Mother mirrored that teacher.

In her final years of teaching Mother focused on remedial reading, helping those students struggling to comprehend the written word. She loved to read, rarely turned off the light next to bed at night without reading for a while, and wanted all students to know that pleasure.

And then there was her role as a grandmother – how she loved it! Wendy presented her with three grandchildren - Carrie, Sean and Tom, and Don and I added two more - Martha and Seth. She loved each of them dearly, openly expressing that love to them.

...

She left us too soon – just days before her sixty-third birthday.

Mother was at home until the final five days of her life when she was hospitalized in Rochester. Wendy and I, our husbands, Richard and Don, and our families had been home on a weekend and we adults had attended a school reunion. Dad, too, had taken a few hours to attend the open house and chat with some of his classmates. It must have been difficult for him to say over and over that his wife was coming to the end of her life. That Sunday afternoon, Wendy and I went to see Mother at the hospital. We found her only semi-lucid. In the car on the way back to Stewartville, Wendy said out loud what I, too, had been thinking – "that we might never see Mother again."

The next morning, I was ironing when the phone rang and Dad informed me that the doctor had told him that he didn't expect Mother to live out the day. I remember asking if he wanted me to come (it was a two and a half hour drive), but he said no.

It was only a few hours later that he called to say she was gone. We packed the car and drove to Stewartville. It was dusk when we arrived and Dad was sitting on the back patio. He and I embraced for a moment (something we didn't do easily at that time) and I could see he was glad that we were there.

The house held a strange stillness. Mother's absence was sharply felt.

Wendy, Richard and their family arrived that night, too.

During the next few days we went through the motions of living - making funeral plans and greeting family and friends.

In the corner of the dining room, on the black-painted captain's chair, sat Mother's purse - a large, white, soft "marshmallow" bag. It remained there for days. No one touched it. I wasn't in the habit of going through Mother's purse, and I think I half expected that she would be the one to pick it up.

Eventually, someone went through that purse and sorted out her personal information, and the purse was no longer in the place where Mother normally laid it.

My heart was as empty as that chair.

Chapter 14

My journey has taken me deep into the lives and times of Margaret and Oscar, Carrie and Milton and Mother. I have walked the streets of Lanesboro and have felt their presence with me; I have envisioned Carrie's restaurants and Milton's cigar-making quarters, as well as Margaret's nursing wards. I have revisited in memory, time after time, my childhood home where Margaret lived with us. If not for the papers tied with red cord, I never would have known of the dark sides of their lives.

…

Margaret - my name.

Knowing the hardship that my great-great grandmother, Margaret Fowler Dent, faced as a young widow with seven children, and that my grandmother, Margaret Dent, bore as a silent mother, I will wear my name proudly. It was a name passed in love that honors two women - two women who must have mustered incredible strength to bear what life dealt them.

Chapter 15

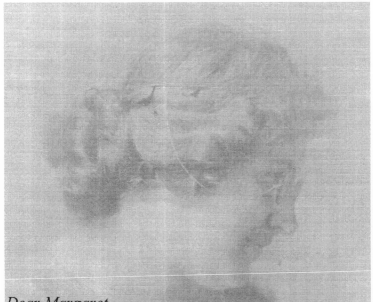

Dear Margaret,
I only knew you as the bed-ridden "aunt" who resided in the small middle bedroom at our house. Six decades separate our time together, but, after delving into your story, I now feel a bond with you.
Margaret, I am deeply saddened that you had to live a life of shame and guilt when you had the right to be openly proud and acknowledge the woman you created – my mother.

I have unfairly judged you, your father, and your siblings from a few long-ago written letters. Forgive me for that.

I have laid your life bare and have made public letters that were meant to be personal, but at last, you, and Mother, too, have voices.

I understand the reason for the angry, condemning letters you wrote to your father. Instead of showing you love at a time in your life when you truly needed it, he cast you away. I also recognize that you had to have lived a lonely life. Moving from state institution to state institution, never having a home of your own, and constantly dealing with patients had to have been very difficult.

I choose to believe that, despite your illnesses, your final years in our household were happy years for you: You finally were able to be with your daughter.

While the moral code of your era made it impossible for you claim our mother as your daughter, the far-reaching consequences of that code prevented Wendy and me from knowing our relationship to you -

We never got to call you "Grandma."

Love from another Margaret,
Peggy

Acknowledgements

Tying the threads of this story would not have been possible without the resources of the Fillmore County Museum, Fountain, Minnesota; the Minnesota History Center, St. Paul; the E.T. Barnard Research Library at the Otter Tail (MN) Historical Society; a video, *A Historical Documentary of AH-GWAH-CHING Sanitorium, 1907-1961*; *Nursing 1910 Style* by Diane Sussman, Nurseweek magazine, Dec. 23, 1999; *Kirkbride Buildings – Historic Insane Asylums*, www.kirkbridebuildings.com, and Ancestry.com.

I am indebted to my fellow writers in the Rivertown Writers: Pat Hanson, Jane Holsteen, Marlene Cox, Penny Smith, Mary Louise Olson, and Margarita Hendrickson, as well as those in the Riverside Writers: Pat Hanson, Mary Wicker, Joan Simpson, Diana Swanson, Alison Baker, Judy Gorfain, Phyllis Langseth, Vicki Anderson and Lois Duffy. They listened, offered insight and encouraged me to commit this story to paper.

For his love, support, and patience, I sincerely thank my husband, Don. Because.

Lastly, I acknowledge that this story would not have come to light without the memories of family members, and, of course, the bundle of letters and papers – tied with red cord.

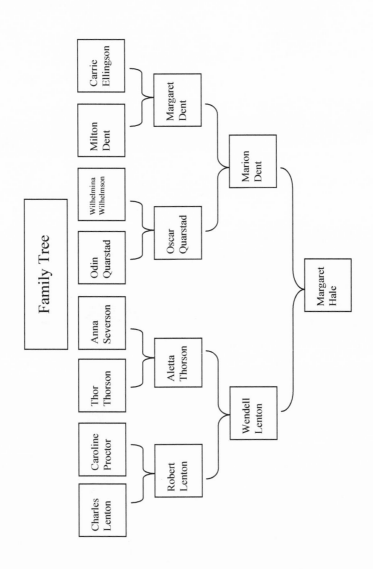

26052850R00122

Made in the USA
Lexington, KY
15 September 2013